*FAMOUS KINGS
AND EMPERORS*

BRIEF BIOGRAPHIES

Famous Explorers

Famous Composers

Brief Biographies

Famous Kings and Emperors

Theodore Rowland-Entwistle
and
Jean Cooke

DAVID & CHARLES

NEWTON ABBOT LONDON NORTH POMFRET (VT) VANCOUVER

ISBN 0 7153 7240 8

Library of Congress Catalog Card Number: 76-40622

Set in 11 on 13pt Garamond
and printed in Great Britain
by Latimer Trend & Company Ltd Plymouth
for David & Charles (Publishers) Limited
Brunel House   Newton Abbot   Devon

Published in the United States of America
by David & Charles Inc
North Pomfret   Vermont 05053   USA

Published in Canada
by Douglas David & Charles Limited
1875 Welch Street   North Vancouver   BC

FOREWORD

History contains the names of many kings, emperors and other rulers, some great, some insignificant. This book contains a selection of those who have been judged most important, either for what they were or for what they did—or did not do. They range from such world conquerors as Alexander the Great and Napoleon I to the boy-king Tutankhamun of Egypt, whose grave, because of his relative unimportance, survived to show us today the true splendour of Ancient Egypt.

By convention, most English-language reference books give the anglicised form of monarchs' names, so for the sake of ease of reference from and to other books we have followed suit. Thus the French Henri and the German Heinrich both appear as Henry.

Although the title of this book refers to 'Kings and Emperors' only, it includes queens and empresses too, and the terms 'king' and 'emperor' must be taken as referring to the office and not to the sex of the office-holder. It was, after all, Elizabeth I who said: 'I have the heart and stomach of a king, and of a king of England too.'

T.R-E.
J.C.

AKBAR THE GREAT (1542–1605), emperor of India, was the greatest ruler of the Mughal Empire, which was founded by his grandfather, BABAR. Under his rule—contemporary with the Elizabethan age in England—a small kingdom based precariously on Delhi expanded to cover 15 provinces, comprising most of present-day India, Pakistan and Bangladesh.

Akbar succeeded his father, Humayun, when he was only 13 years old. Humayun had just recaptured a small part of the Mughal Empire which had been taken by Afghan conquerors. Akbar, guided at first by his guardian, Bairam Khan, set out to conquer the lands around him. In a series of campaigns he extended his dominion over the Indian sub-continent. Warfare lasted until 1600, but even then Akbar had further plans. His last years were saddened by a rebellion by his son, Jahangir.

Akbar was a vigorous, energetic man, passionately fond of sport, and quick in action. He drank heavily, though was not a drunkard like many others of his family. He could not read or write, having as a boy dodged his lessons in favour of sport, but he was exceptionally clear-headed, and knew how to take his time in making important policy decisions. Akbar was a mystic. He was brought up as a strict Muslim, but in later life deviated from the faith of his fathers. He held a series of religious debates in which Muslims, Hindus and Portuguese Jesuit priests took part, after which he formed a new religion of his own, called the Divine Faith with which he intended to unite different creeds; but he did not inflict it on other people. Akbar reformed the administration of his empire, and particularly the methods by which taxes were raised. He encouraged music, writing and painting, and under his direction many temples, public buildings and forts were erected.

AKHENATEN (*c.* 1392 BC–*c.* 1362 BC), pharaoh of Egypt, was a religious fanatic who tried to alter his country's official religion. He was named *Amenhotep* after his father, Amenhotep III, a name

7

that means 'the peace of Amun'. Amun-Re was the king of the many gods that the Egyptians then worshipped. Akhenaten's mother, Tiy, brought him up to revere the Sun-disc, the Aten, as a universal god.

Akhenaten became pharaoh at the age of 13 on the death of his father, and assumed the title Amenhotep IV. Encouraged by his mother, the young king supported the cult of Aten and discouraged that of Amun-Re. He built new temples for the Sun-god at Karnak, and encouraged new forms of art and literature based on a natural approach. Earlier statues of pharaohs were stylised and all tended to look alike: Akhenaten's reign produced sculptures that looked like their subjects. Among many that have survived is the well-known portrait-bust of Akhenaten's wife, Queen Nefertiti.

About 1374 BC Akhenaten took a drastic step to remove his court from the powerful priesthood of Amun-Re. He moved his capital from Thebes to a new city some 300 miles (480km) further north, which he named Akhetaten, 'Horizon of Aten'. Soon afterwards he changed his own name to Akhenaten. As time went on the followers of Amun were persecuted, and the pharaoh permitted worship of only one god, the Aten. Akhenaten spent so much of his time and energy in religious reform that he neglected the administration of the country, and portions of the Egyptian empire in Syria were seized by the Hittites. By the time the pharaoh was 30 his lack of firm government had brought his kingdom almost to disaster. With his health failing rapidly, Akhenaten married his daughter, Meritaten, to a nobleman named Smenkhkare and named him as heir. About a year after Akhenaten's death Smenkhkare died or was deposed, and Tutankhaten, husband of Meritaten's younger sister Ankhsenpaaten, became pharaoh. Soon afterwards he changed his name to TUTANKHAMUN, and the court returned to Thebes and the worship of Amun-Re.

ALBERT I (1875–1934), king of the Belgians, succeeded his uncle, Leopold II, in 1909. He spent his years as heir to the throne in the Belgian army and travelling abroad. His military background was soon put to the test on the outbreak of World War I in 1914: the German government demanded that Belgium should allow German forces to pass through its country in order to attack France. The Belgian Parliament refused, and on 4 August German troops invaded the country. Albert took command of his troops, and fought a fierce rearguard action until the army reached the river Yser. Throughout the war he remained with the army, sharing its dangers and discomforts; and in the final Allied offensive of October 1918, Albert commanded a combined French and Belgian army which recaptured Ostend and Bruges.

Albert interested himself in social and other reforms in the years after the war, and also in the fortunes of the Belgian Congo (now Zaire). Among his recreations was rock-climbing, a fall bringing his death in the Ardennes. Albert married Elisabeth, daughter of the Duke of Bavaria; he was succeeded by his elder son, Leopold III.

ALEXANDER THE GREAT (356 BC–323 BC), king of Macedonia, in Greece, became the first of the world-conquerors: his empire at its height stretching from Greece in the west to the Indus valley in the east.

His father, Philip of Macedonia, was a warrior-king who ruled over one of the small states that made up ancient Greece. His mother, Olympias, the daughter of a king of Epirus, was said to be descended from Achilles and from Zeus, the king of the Greek gods. On the night before her wedding she dreamed she was mating with Zeus, and she always believed that Alexander was of divine origin; many people indeed regarded Alexander as a god, even in his own lifetime.

Philip spent most of his time fighting, and Alexander was brought up by his mother and by the great philosopher Aristotle, who was engaged as his tutor. Alexander studied literature and philosophy, and was an accomplished musician, but he also excelled in outdoor and warlike activities. Alexander envied his father's prowess as a warrior, and feared there would be nothing left for him to conquer. Father and son quarrelled when Philip took a second wife and made her queen. But soon afterwards Philip was murdered, and Alexander became king, as Alexander III, at the age of 20.

The first thing he faced was a revolt by a group of Greek city-states that were under Macedonian rule. The group—the League of Corinth—was led by the city of Thebes. By swift action Alexander defeated the rebels, and laid Thebes waste.

With Greece under his sway, Alexander turned his attention to an old ambition of his father's—the conquest of Persia. In the spring of 334 BC he led an invading army 35,000 strong across the Hellespont (the Dardanelles). A much larger Persian army met him on the banks of the river Granicus, near the Sea of Marmara. Leading his cavalry, Alexander crushed his opponents in a swift, fierce battle and found himself at a stroke master of Asia Minor (modern Turkey in Asia). He quickly subdued a number of Persian strongholds, including Gordium, capital of Phrygia. The following year he encountered an even stronger Persian force, led this time by its king, Darius III. At the battle of Issus Alexander routed Darius, and captured the Persian camp with Darius's wife and mother.

In the year 332 BC Alexander marched southwards down the Phoenician coast, capturing the cities of Tyre and Gaza, and rode unopposed across the Sinai Desert into Egypt, then a Persian province. There he was hailed as pharaoh as he set about re-organising the country's government. He realised that Egypt needed a port, so he founded one, the city of Alexandria.

The following year he turned eastwards to attack the Persians once more. Darius had assembled an even larger army to oppose him, and had chosen the spot on which to fight, on level ground near Arbela, east of the river Tigris. The Macedonian army was greatly outnumbered, but by leading a charge directly at Darius himself Alexander made the king flee for his life, and the Persian army broke up. Alexander proceeded to capture the main cities of the Persian empire, including Babylon and Persepolis. Darius fled into Media, on the shores of the Caspian Sea. Alexander and a small party chased after him, but when they finally caught up with Darius he was dying, murdered by his own people.

Alexander spent the next few years consolidating his conquests and quelling several revolts among his followers. In 327 BC he led his armies eastwards once more, this time over the Hindu Kush mountain range to India. He had only reached the valley of the river Indus, now in Pakistan, when his war-weary troops would follow him no further, and he was forced to agree to return. He did so by sailing down the Indus and marching west-wards through the coastal deserts, where he lost many of his followers.

Alexander settled down in Babylon, his chosen capital, and set to work to administer his vast empire. He married a Persian princess (one of his several wives) and encouraged his officers to marry Persians too. He reformed the currency and set up good trading and communications systems. Then, just as he was organising an expedition to conquer Arabia, he contracted malaria, and within 10 days he was dead. He was 32 years and 8 months old.

ALFRED THE GREAT (849–899), king of Wessex, was the greatest of the Saxon kings of England. He was the youngest of the 5 sons of King Ethelwulf, and grandson of Egbert, the first king to claim supremacy over all England. As a small boy he went twice to Rome, the second time on a pilgrimage with his father. The culture and learning of Rome impressed him, and decided him to become a scholar.

When Ethelwulf died in 858 his eldest son was already dead, and he was succeeded by his second son, Ethelbald, a religious man who died after only 2 years as king. The third son, Ethelbert, reigned for about 5 years before he, too, died. At the time the fourth brother, Ethelred I, became king the country faced a massive invasion from the Danes. These Northmen, as they were known, had harried England from time to time, but departed after each raid. This time they arrived in force with the intention of staying. Within 4 years they had captured the kingdoms of Northumbria, Mercia, and East Anglia, and controlled all England north of the river Thames.

Alfred, a loyal supporter of each of his brothers, had to abandon his books for the sword. As second in command to Ethelred he took part in 5 battles in 871. Early on Alfred showed his initiative by leading a lightning attack on the Danes while Ethelred was still at his morning devotions. This victory at Ashdown, near Reading, was followed by a series of defeats. In the middle of the campaign Ethelred died and Alfred became king. He fought 4 more battles that year before he was able to buy off the Danes for the winter by paying a ransom, or *danegeld*. The Danes left Wessex alone for a few years while they consolidated their conquests in the north. During this respite Alfred built up the Saxon fleet, and used it to drive off part of the Danish fleet.

In the winter of 877-8 the Danes made a fresh onslaught on Wessex, ravaging the land. Alfred and a handful of followers had to seek refuge in the Isle of Athelney, a hill amid marshland in Somerset. There he is said to have taken shelter in a peasant woman's cottage and watched her cakes cooking. Further details of this story are later inventions. When spring came Alfred roused his followers and marched out to meet and defeat the Danes at the battle of Edington. The Danes under their king, Guthrum, were forced to surrender. Alfred was magnanimous, offering his enemies peace and a treaty that split England between Danes and Saxons. North-east of a line from the Mersey to the Thames was the *Danelaw*; south-west lay Wessex and part of Mercia under Saxon rule. At first London lay in the Danelaw, but following a Danish invasion of Kent in 885 Alfred captured it.

Having achieved peace, Alfred devoted his energies not only to preserving it, but to making the best use of it. He created a strong army and navy, for defence and not conquest. He also led the way to reviving England's scholarship and literature, bringing in scholars to Wessex from less affected parts of England, Wales, and Continental Europe. He set up a school for the young nobles of his court, and taught in it himself. He translated many works into Old English from Latin, then the main language of scholarship. His philosophy may be summed up in his own words: 'Wisdom is of such kind that no man of this world can conceive of her as she really is, but each strives according to the measure of his wit to understand her if he may, for wisdom is of God.'

ASHURBANIPAL (died *c.* 626 BC), the grandson of SENNACHERIB, was the last of the great kings of Assyria. He was a man of all-round ability, a great soldier, a scholar and a hunter. He succeeded his father, Esarhaddon, in about 669 BC, just as Esarhaddon was in the middle of conquering Egypt. Ashurbanipal began his reign by consolidating Assyrian power in Egypt, capturing Thebes, and making an Egyptian prince, Necho, his viceroy. A revolt by the Egyptians 7 years later caused Ashurbanipal to exact obedience and inflict punishment. He destroyed Thebes and pacified the country.

In 652 BC Ashurbanipal was attacked by his brother Shamash-shum-ukin, king of Babylon. But the revolt was badly organised, and Ashurbanipal marched swiftly into Babylonia, besieging its chief cities. Shamash-shum-ukin, despairing of success, set fire to Babylon and died in the flames. Ashurbanipal inflicted a fearful revenge on Shamash-shum-ukin's allies, and took 2 kings back to his capital, Nineveh, where he chained them in kennels in front of his palace gates, like dogs. He also appears to have taken the king of Judah, Manasseh, prisoner on suspicion of aiding Shamash-shum-ukin.

All these campaigns exhausted the strength of Assyria, and though Ashurbanipal held a Triumph (a victory celebration) in 642 BC, he no longer had the ability to retake Egypt when that country rebelled yet again. Between 642 BC and his death about 626 BC there is little record of events in Assyria, but the empire must have been disintegrating rapidly, because it broke up finally within a few years of his death.

Ashurbanipal collected a large library, inscribed on clay tablets. It was discovered in the 1850s in the ruins of his palace at Nineveh, and contained copies of texts that were already 1,400 years old in Ashurbanipal's time. It also included an account of his reign down to 642 BC.

ASOKA (died *c.* 232 BC) was the third and greatest of the Maurya emperors of India, a dynasty founded by his grandfather Chandragupta Maurya. He became emperor on the death of his father, Bindusara, in about 274 BC, although he had to fight for the throne, and legend says that he won it after killing many of his brothers. In his first years on the throne he extended the already sizeable empire he had inherited, so that it stretched from Kabul (now in Afghanistan) in the north-west to Nepal in the north-east, and southward to cover most of the Indian peninsula.

About 8 years after he became emperor, Asoka became sickened by the misery caused by war. He abandoned the Hindu faith and became a Buddhist, devoting the rest of his life to the propagation of Buddhism and the moral reform of his empire. His policies were based on *ahimsa* (non-violence) and *maitri* (friendliness), which he applied to all living creatures. He appointed censors of morals and religion, though he preached religious toleration, organising charity and justice. He stressed the necessity for parental obedience, treating animals and servants kindly, and leading a simple life. Though he preached the tenets of Buddhism, he did not oppress Hinduism, and indeed claimed to have helped to spread it among the pagan tribes of the jungles.

His son Mahinda is said to have converted Ceylon to Buddhism, and he also sent missionaries and envoys to lands outside his empire, though with little apparent success. The effects of his policies inside the empire are hard to assess, but Asoka's name was venerated for many generations by his people. His enthusiasm for Buddhism encouraged its spread as a major religion. After his death his policies lapsed, and the Maurya empire fell to pieces.

ATAHUALPA (*c*. 1500–1533) was the last of the Inca emperors who ruled in Peru. His father was the emperor Huayna Capac, who on his deathbed is said to have prophesied that the strange white men who were rumoured to be invading the land would cause the end of the Inca empire. Huayna Capac had a legitimate son, Huascar, by his queen, and many illegitimate sons by his concubines. His favourite son was one of these, Atahualpa. Huascar became emperor when his father died, while Atahualpa became king of Quito. The half-brothers remained at peace for 5 years, but in 1530 they quarrelled and civil war broke out. By 1532 Huascar was imprisoned, and Atahualpa had made himself emperor.

His success was short lived, for the Spanish *conquistador* Francisco Pizarro was already marching towards the Inca empire in search of gold and territory. Pizarro sent a captured Indian to Atahualpa as an envoy, and in due course received a friendly reply. On 15 November 1532 Pizarro and his force, which consisted of only about 180 men, met Atahualpa in the Inca city of Cajamarca. Atahualpa had more than 3,000 followers, mostly unarmed. The Spaniards called on Atahualpa to become a Christian and to acknowledge the Spanish ruler, Charles V, as his overlord. The Inca ruler not unnaturally replied that he would not. At a signal from Pizarro the Spaniards, armed with guns and swords, fell on the defenceless Incas, slaughtering many of them and capturing Atahualpa.

Atahualpa was treated with courtesy by the Spaniards. He soon discovered that gold was what they wanted, and decided to buy his freedom. He offered Pizarro to fill a large room 9ft deep with gold objects, which would take 2 months to collect. While this was going on Atahualpa gave secret orders for the execution of Huascar, whom he feared might side with the Spaniards to overthrow him. The treasure duly arrived, but Atahualpa remained a prisoner. Finally, the Spaniards brought him to trial on a number of spurious charges, such as murdering his brother, having more than one wife and squandering the country's revenues. They found him guilty and condemned him to be burned at the stake, but commuted this to strangulation when Atahualpa in his last minutes of life agreed to be baptised a Christian.

ATTILA (*c.* 406–453) was king of the Huns, a nomadic tribe of Mongols who had established an empire in eastern Europe, stretching from the Baltic Sea to the Caspian Sea. He became joint ruler with his elder brother Bleda on the death of their uncle, Rua, in 433. The Huns demanded a large annual subsidy from the Eastern Roman Empire. When this was not forthcoming they attacked the empire, capturing and destroying many cities, including Belgrade and Sofia. When the Romans finally secured peace they had to pay treble the amount of gold each year. Atilla's activities earned him the name in Roman circles of 'the Scourge of God'.

In 445 Attila murdered Bleda and made himself absolute ruler. Soon afterwards Honoria, sister of the western Roman emperor Valentinian III, asked Attila's aid to escape from an unwelcome marriage. Attila promptly led a large force of barbarians westwards across the river Rhine into Gaul, claiming Honoria as his own bride. He was defeated by a combined Roman and Visigoth (German) army at Châlons-sur-Marne in 451. This crucial battle checked the Hun invasion of Europe.

Attila's army, though defeated, remained intact, and he at once changed course and marched into Italy, ravaging the countryside. He ignored personal appeals by Pope Leo I and others to spare Rome, but heeded a much more cogent argument: plague coupled with shortage of food. He retreated north of the Alps, and prepared to make a fresh attack on the Eastern Roman empire. In 453 he married a German girl named Idilco, and died on his wedding night. His sons divided his empire, and quarrelled among themselves. Within 50 years the Huns had ceased to be a power to be reckoned with.

AUGUSTUS (63 BC–AD 14) was the first of the Roman emperors. He was the great-nephew of Julius Caesar, who had adopted him as his heir. Augustus was named *Gaius Octavianus*, and in his early years he is generally referred to as Octavian. He was a 19-year-old student at Apollonia, in what is now Albania, when Caesar died. He immediately returned to Italy to claim his inheritance, and adopted Caesar's names as well as his own. At first he was opposed by Caesar's friend Marcus Antonius (Mark Antony), but he raised an army and defeated Antony. The two then formed an alliance, and later in 43 BC, with an unimportant general named Aemilius Lepidus, they formed a triumvirate to rule the territories of Rome.

One of the first tasks of Octavian and Antony was to seek out and defeat Caesar's murderers. They then divided the Roman provinces between them, Octavian ruling in the west and Antony in the east. Lepidus was assigned to Africa, but was later deposed. The alliance between Antony and Octavian was further strengthened when Antony married Octavian's sister, Octavia. But the rivalry between the 2 men was obvious, and Octavian spent the next few years building up his strength and popularity and waiting for a chance to deal with his rival.

Antony played into his hands by deserting Octavia and falling hopelessly in love with Cleopatra, the beautiful and ruthless queen of Egypt. When the triumvirate came to the end of its official term in office in 32 BC, Octavian called on Antony to resign. Antony declined and, as his affair with Cleopatra had made him unpopular in Rome, Octavian had no difficulty in leading an army against him. The Roman fleet defeated the ships of Antony and Cleopatra at the battle of Actium in 31 BC, and soon afterwards the unhappy lovers committed suicide. Octavian, at the age of 33, was master of the Roman empire.

For several years his power was real rather than official, his position being merely that of one of the 2 consuls who exercised power, and were elected annually. Then in 27 BC he agreed to give up the additional powers he had exercised ever since the war against Antony. The Roman Senate promptly responded by voting him full dictatorial powers, and giving him the title *Augustus*—'exalted'. The new powers were temporary, and to be exercised within the constitution of the Roman Republic. Augustus was solemnly re-elected consul every year, though he was ruler of a huge province comprising Gaul, Spain, Syria, and Egypt. Finally, under pressure from the public, the Senate gave him the rank of consul for life, and from then on he was effectively emperor.

For a century Rome had been torn by civil war, so the strong rule of Augustus provided the best chance of a return to law and order. He reformed the government, setting up a rough and ready form of administration responsible to himself. Among other reforms were the formation of a fire brigade, better taxation systems, an efficient postal service, and the establishment of a standing army. He paid particular attention to Rome's morals, passing laws against adultery and reviving the worship of the gods.

The city of Rome itself benefited greatly from his work. He boasted, truthfully: 'I found Rome built of sun-dried bricks; I leave her built of marble'. Roads were restored and repaved, temples rebuilt and many public buildings erected. Augustus encouraged the arts, particularly poetry. He was assiduous in the administration of justice. Even before his death many people revered him as a god—a cult he did his best to discourage.

Augustus was a handsome man, bright-eyed and always calm. He was fond of women and gambling, but though he lived in an age of luxury his own tastes were simple. He gave many formal banquets, but ate sparingly himself. Above all he had a statesman-like gift of being able to persuade people to do as he wanted, and of guiding public opinion. The empire he created lasted for several hundred years.

AURANGZEB (1618–1707) was the last of the Mughal emperors of India. He was the third son of SHAH JAHAN by his wife Mumtaz Mahal. As a young man he held a series of governorships and viceroyalties in his father's extensive domains. The last of these appointments was as viceroy of the Deccan, in the southern part of his father's domains, which he attempted to extend further south by conquest.

In 1657 Shah Jahan fell seriously ill, and Aurangzeb at once marched north to seize power. His brothers opposed him but he defeated them, imprisoned his father, and declared himself emperor.

Aurangzeb was a religious fanatic of a narrow, puritanical mind. He allowed his strict Muslim ideas to override his many other qualities, which included courage, clear-headedness, and great industry. He ended the religious toleration of preceding reigns, and oppressed the Hindu people under his rule. He destroyed their temples and taxed them heavily. This led to widespread discontent and rebellion.

Although Aurangzeb was able to extend his empire to its furthest extent, its economy and administration gradually decayed. He spent the first part of his reign in the north, while his officers mismanaged affairs in the south. Then he moved to the south while the north gradually went to pieces. By the time he died at the age of 89 there was nobody he could trust, and during the next few years the Mughal Empire disintegrated.

BABAR (1483–1530) was the first Mughal ruler of India. He was part Turkish and part Mongol by birth, and was a descendant of GENGHIS KHAN and TAMERLANE. His name at first was *Zahir ud-Din*. At the age of 11 he succeeded his father as ruler of Fergana, a petty kingdom in Turkistan, but lost it after a long struggle. At the age of 21 he made himself ruler of Kabul, the modern capital of Afghanistan. From this vantage point he led a series of raids over the mountains into India. His boldness earned him fame and fortune. In 1522 the governor of Lahore asked Babar's help against his overlord, the Sultan of Delhi.

Babar led an army of 8,000 men into India, to be confronted by a force of 50,000 plus 1,000 elephants. But Babar had guns, and at the battle of Panipat in 1526 he destroyed his opponents and made himself master of Delhi and its territory. The following year he defeated an army of petty kings to the south—again overcoming huge odds—and in 1529 he defeated the Afghan rulers of Bengal. Soon afterwards his eldest son, Humayun, lay dying. Babar followed an old custom and at a religious ceremony formally offered his own life in exchange for that of his son. Humayun recovered, and Babar, whose health was failing, died shortly afterwards.

BELSHAZZAR (died 539 BC) was the crown prince of Babylon, and co-ruler of the city with his father Nabonidus. He was probably the grandson of NEBUCHADREZZAR II, although the Bible refers to him as Nebuchadrezzar's son. Nabonidus became king of Babylon in 556 BC and about 6 years later led an army to a distant part of Arabia, leaving Belshazzar to rule the city. In 539 BC the Persian armies of CYRUS THE GREAT entered the city, which they captured without much of a fight. According to both the Bible and the Greek historian Xenophon, Belshazzar was holding a lavish feast when the Persians walked in. Belshazzar apparently died in the skirmishing, while his father was captured soon afterwards while leading his army to recapture Babylon.

BORIS GODUNOV (*c.* 1551–1605) was elected Tsar of All the Russias in 1598, having ruled the country in all but name for the previous 14 years. Boris Godunov was a member of an old Russian family in whose veins ran Tartar blood—his ancestors were members of the Golden Horde, a Mongol kingdom in southern Russia. He entered the service of the tsar IVAN THE TERRIBLE, that strange mixture of religious fanatic and bloodthirsty madman who slew his eldest son in a fit of rage. Following this disaster the succession fell to Ivan's younger son, Fedor, who married Boris's sister Irina. Ivan appointed Boris as one of the guardians of Fedor, who was feeble both in body and mind.

Ivan died in 1584 and Fedor became tsar. Boris was co-regent with another nobleman until 1585, when he became sole regent. Boris proved a wise and capable minister. Under his rule the country enjoyed a rare period of peace and prosperity. But in 1597 he issued a decree by which peasants were tied to the land on which they worked. Thus serfdom began in Russia, and made millions of hitherto free people virtually slaves. Boris did this to win the support of the smaller landowners, who suffered from a shortage of labour.

When Fedor died in 1598 his widow was proclaimed tsaritsa. She at once retired to a convent and a national assembly offered the crown to Boris, who thus became tsar by election. He proved to be quite as ruthless as any other of the Russian tsars who had preceded him, but his ruthlessness was not so obvious or so bloodthirsty as that of Ivan the Terrible. Boris relied a good deal on informers, however, and put to death or exiled anyone who appeared to oppose him. He encouraged relations with western Europe, particularly with the English, Dutch, French and Germans.

Just before his death a rebellion broke out, supported by the king of Poland. It was headed by a pretender claiming to be Dmitri, half-brother and heir of Fedor, who had died mysteriously in exile in 1591. Some historians believe that Boris had the true Dmitri killed, but others believe his death was natural. When Boris died in 1605, a period known as 'The Time of Troubles' began; his young son, the tsar Fedor, was murdered after a few months; the false Dmitri became tsar and was then murdered; and not until a new tsar was elected in 1612 did Russia find peace again.

BRIAN BORU (*c.* 940–1014) was the most powerful of the High Kings of Ireland. He was the son of Cennedige (Kennedy), prince of Dál Chais, a small state in eastern Clare. Brian's half-brother, Mathgamain (Mahon) became king of Munster, one of the four Provinces of Ireland in 964, and when he was murdered in 976 Brian succeeded him. Brian's first task was to avenge his brother, who had been killed by the Eoganachta sept, previous holders of the throne of Munster. He achieved this in a series of battles, also defeating the Vikings, then busy raiding Ireland.

Brian's wise rule united Munster and made it a strong kingdom. This and his growing ambition led him into a headlong clash with Maelsechlainn, the Ard Rí (High King) of all Ireland. In 1002 Brian replaced Maelsechlainn, and all the other rulers of Ireland submitted to him. However, rebellion eventually broke out, the people of Leinster joining forces with the Vikings. Brian's army, led by his son, encountered the Vikings at Clontarf, near Dublin, on Good Friday, 1014, in one of the greatest battles ever fought in Ireland. It ended in victory for Brian's forces, but the aged king was surprised by a small band of Vikings and hacked to pieces. The battle of Clontarf ended Viking power in Ireland.

CATHERINE II, THE GREAT (1729–1796), was a German princess who became Empress of Russia. She was the daughter of Prince Christian of Anhalt-Zerbst, and was named Sophia Augusta Frederica. On her betrothal to Peter, the heir to the Russian throne, she adopted the name Catherine and also the Eastern Orthodox religion. Catherine was a witty and highly-educated girl of 16 when she married; her husband was callous and stupid, and she despised him. The Russian court was dissolute, but until she was 25 Catherine remained faithful. Then she took the first of a series of lovers, and quickly became notorious.

Peter became emperor in 1762 on the death of his aunt, the Empress Elizabeth. Half-German himself, he admired all things German, and especially the ruler of Prussia, FREDERICK THE GREAT. His behaviour, and his avowed intention to divorce Catherine, led her many friends to decide he must be removed. Six months after his accession, a *coup d'état* by a group of army officers deposed Peter and Catherine was proclaimed empress in his place. A few weeks later Peter mysteriously died in a scuffle with 2 of the empress's friends.

In spite of the highly dubious means by which Catherine came to power, her accession was a good thing for Russia as she was a conscientious and able ruler, pursuing her own foreign policy with considerable success. By a mixture of military success and cunning diplomacy Catherine extended Russia's frontiers to include a large part of Poland, and captured the Crimea and the Black Sea coast from Turkey.

In home affairs Catherine strengthened the power of the nobles at the expense of the peasants; a series of revolts being put down in a barbarous manner. She also instituted reforms in agriculture, education and medicine. She took her rôle as ruler seriously, rising at 5am every day and working for 15 hours. All state papers were not only read but carefully annotated. In addition to her official work, she was a tireless letter-writer and a brilliant conversationalist. She encouraged art, science and literature, and herself studied and wrote history. She had many lovers, but never allowed herself to be influenced by them in important matters. When she died of an apoplectic fit in 1796 she was succeeded by her son, Paul I, who was very much the son of his father, Peter III, and devoted much of his time to reversing every reform that his mother had introduced.

CHARLEMAGNE (742–814) was King of the Franks, and later made himself Emperor of the West. By so doing he revived the Roman empire, defunct since 476, and founded an empire—later known as the Holy Roman Empire—which lasted until NAPOLEON I destroyed it in 1806.

Charlemagne is a French version of *Carolus Magnus*—Charles the Great—a title which helps to distinguish him from the many other rulers named Charles in European history. Charles was the son of Pepin the Short, King of the Franks, whose kingdom covered France, the Low Countries and parts of modern Germany and Austria. When Pepin died he divided his lands between his two sons, Charles and Carloman. Charles had the western part and Carloman the east. The 2 brothers hated each other, but before this hatred could flare into civil war Carloman died in 771 at the age of 20, apparently from natural causes. Charles became the ruler of the whole kingdom. Carloman's widow and children took refuge in Italy at the court of Desiderius, King of Lombardy. Charles had earlier married Desiderius's daughter, but divorced her within a year, so relations between Charles and Lombardy were already strained.

Desiderius claimed some of the lands ruled by the pope, Adrian I, whereupon the pope appealed to Charles for aid. Charles responded by leading two armies into Italy and over-throwing Desiderius, who spent the rest of his life as a monk. Charles made himself king of Lombardy. Charles fought a long series of campaigns, in the course of which he subdued the Saxons and the Bavarians. The Saxon wars lasted for 30 years, ending in final victory in 797.

To the south, Charles feared attacks from the Moorish (Muslim) rulers of Spain, and in 778 he led an expedition into Spain over the Pyrenees. He seized territory including the cities of Barcelona and Pamplona, and organised it as part of his kingdom. Then he retired north into France again. At the pass of Roncesvalles a force of Basques, who fancied Frankish rule as little as they liked Moorish rule, fell on Charles's rearguard and butchered them in a day-long fight. Among the many dead was one Hruoland, Warden of the Breton March, who as Roland became the subject of countless medieval legends and songs. The Basques vanished before Charles returned to help his rearguard, and in spite of what legend says he was unable to avenge the slaughter.

In 799 a new pope, Leo III, was elected. Soon afterwards Leo's enemies accused him of gross crimes and immoralities. He fled for safety to Charles's deputy in Rome, the Duke of Spoleto. Charles summoned the pope to him at Paderborn, in north-western Germany, where he held a secret and highly irregular trial of the accused pontiff. He found Leo not guilty and sent him back to Rome. There he joined him at the end of 800 and held a new trial, at which Leo was confronted with his accusers. The falsity of the charges was completely proved. Two days later Charles attended Christmas Day Mass in St Peter's Basilica. There Leo crowned him as Emperor of the West. According to some historians, the act came as a surprise to Charles, but others believe that it was carefully planned by him beforehand.

The rest of his reign was comparatively peaceful and Charles spent the greater part of his time reorganising the administration of his empire. He replaced direct taxation of his nobles by services in return for grants of land—the basis of the later feudal system. He delegated a great deal of power in this way, at the same time providing a strong framework for the maintenance of law and order.

Even so, much of the success of the government depended on the personality of Charles himself. He was a tall, athletic man, at least 6ft 4in (2m) in height, with blue eyes, tawny hair and a broad, cheerful face. He was apparently impervious to fatigue. He was a great admirer and patron of learning. He founded an academy at Aachen, his capital. It was for many years under the direction of an English scholar, Alcuin of York. The king himself studied in it from time to time. He was a keen scholar, a tireless letter-writer and a poet. The hymn *Veni, Creator Spiritus* is attributed to him. Only in the art of calligraphy, the superfine penmanship that Alcuin taught, did Charles fail, and from this comes the legend that he could not write. The Aachen school and others Charles founded survived him, and marked the beginning of the long revival of learning that flowered in the 1400s with the Renaissance.

CHARLES I (1600–1649), King of England and Scotland, was executed by order of the English parliament during the civil war of 1642–51. Charles was a member of the Scottish royal family of Stuart, and the son of JAMES I and VI. He was a small, shy man, with a quiet and courteous manner and a slight stammer. He was a serious-minded person and was highly moral in character, but in matters of state he was lazy and content to leave affairs to others. He was also obstinate: once he had an idea he never changed his mind, this being especially true of his views of government. He believed sincerely that he was king by divine right, and that his will should be law.

Charles succeeded his father in 1625, and married Henrietta, sister of the French king, LOUIS XIII, soon afterwards. The financial affairs of the country were in a bad way: the value of money had fallen, but the king's revenue, out of which he had to finance all the affairs of state as well as his own expenses, had stayed much the same. In order to pay his way Charles had to resort to many kinds of taxes, not all of them strictly legal, and every one unpopular. Parliament protested, so the king ruled without it.

All might have been well if Charles had not tried to impose the Anglican religion on the Presbyterian Scots. This imprudent act led to war and the need for much greater funds. Charles had to recall parliament, which insisted not only on tax reforms, but on the trial and execution of Charles's chief minister, the Earl of Strafford, for treason. A few months later Charles tried to have 5 members of parliament arrested for treason. He failed, and England rapidly split into 2 factions, each arming. In 1642 Charles raised his royal standard at Nottingham, calling on all loyal people to rally round him. This led to civil war.

In the years that followed, Charles became a very fair general and scored some notable victories. But the forces of parliament were too strong for him, and in 1645 Charles was decisively defeated at the battle of Naseby. The following year he fled to Scotland, hoping the Scots would protect him. But they handed him over to representatives of the English parliament. A few months later the parliamentary army seized him. In captivity Charles tried to negotiate favourable terms, but he promised different things to the various parties with whom he was dealing, including the Scots. Eventually the army demanded he should be tried for treason and a specially-constituted court heard the case, pronouncing him guilty, as 'a tyrant, a traitor, a murderer, and a public enemy to the Commonwealth of England'. Three days later he was beheaded. His eldest son, later CHARLES II, was safely in exile in the Netherlands. For the next 11 years England was a republic.

CHARLES II (1630–1685) became King of England in 1660, after a period of republican government known as the Interregnum, although many royalists thought he began his reign in 1649, when his father, CHARLES I, was executed. As a boy in 1646—during the Civil War—he was forced to flee from England and took refuge in the Netherlands. In 1650 he landed in Scotland, where the Presbyterian Scots agreed to accept him as king; he was crowned King of Scotland in 1651. He led an army into England, but 9 months later it was decisively defeated at the battle of Worcester. Charles escaped to France after 40 days in disguise, sheltered by loyal supporters.

Charles was invited back to England in 1660 when the government of that country had fallen into disorder. Like his father, his income was too small to meet the needs of government, let alone his court. But he was one of the cleverest kings that England has ever had, and he knew how to damp down hot tempers and harsh feelings. In 1670 he signed a secret treaty with LOUIS XIV of France, his cousin. In it he promised to declare himself a Roman Catholic, and to support France in a war against the Netherlands. In return, Louis supplied him with funds.

In 1678 Charles faced the most serious crisis of his reign. Its basis was the hatred of many Englishmen for Roman Catholicism. A 'Popish plot' was uncovered, and a great deal of false evidence was laid before Parliament, who became determined to ensure that the crown went only to Protestants. Charles, though he had 14 illegitimate children, had no legitimate ones, and his heir was his brother, James, Duke of York, an avowed Roman Catholic. James fled the country, and Charles had to do some adroit political manoeuvring to prevent Parliament from excluding him from the succession. The last years of Charles's reign were comparatively peaceful.

Charles himself was a complex character. He was a keen scientist, and an active patron of the newly-formed Royal Society. He took an active interest in the affairs of his kingdom, and during the Great Fire which destroyed much of London in 1666 it was his intervention that helped to prevent the flames from spreading even more than they did. His court was devoted to the pursuit of pleasure, and Charles himself had many mistresses, his natural caution preventing him from being influenced by them, just as it stopped him from avowing himself a Roman Catholic until he was within a few minutes of death.

CHARLES V (1500–1558) became King of Spain (as Charles I) in 1516, and Holy Roman Emperor (as Charles V) in 1519. He was a member of the powerful Habsburg family, which controlled the affairs of the Empire for more than 600 years, and he ruled over more lands than any other Habsburg. He was the son of Archduke Philip of Austria, a son of Emperor MAXIMILIAN I, and Joan of Castile, daughter and heir of FERDINAND and ISABELLA of Spain. Philip died in 1506 and Joan, never mentally very stable, became hopelessly mad. Charles was brought up by an aunt at what had been the court of Burgundy. He spoke French as his first language, and from the stiff ceremony of the court he developed a grave manner, allied to strong religious views.

In 1515 Charles came of age and began to rule his father's lands, including Burgundy and most of what is now the Low Countries. The following year Ferdinand died, and since Joan was too insane to rule, the combined thrones of Aragon and Castile came to Charles. They also included rule over Sardinia, Sicily, Naples and the growing Spanish empire in America. Three years later Maximilian died, and Charles inherited his vast lands. He was immediately elected emperor.

Charles was crowned emperor at Aachen in 1520. The follow-

ing year he presided over the Diet of Worms, called to hear
Martin Luther defend his doctrines as a Church reformer. Charles
exiled Luther and forbade the new doctrines. He then passed the
problem over to his younger brother Frederick: Charles had a
war with France to worry about.

The subject of the war was Milan, in Italy, which Francis I of
France controlled and Charles claimed. Fighting began in 1521
and continued until Francis was captured in 1525. Charles fought
four more wars against the French over various territories which
both powers claimed. He also fought several campaigns against
the Turks, who were threatening central Europe.

Religious wars between Roman Catholics and the growing
Protestant movement disrupted the Empire during Charles's
reign, and by the time he was 50 his one thought was to abdicate
and relinquish his responsibilities. He negotiated a marriage between his son and Mary I of England in 1554. Two years later, he
gave up the Spanish throne to his son, who became PHILIP II,
abandoning the Empire to his brother, Ferdinand I. He retired
to a monastery in Spain, leading a quiet life, but not taking
religious vows until his death in 1558.

CHARLES XII (1682–1718), King of Sweden, was a bold and
brilliant general who led his country to a series of victories,
followed by equally disastrous defeats, in the Northern War of
1700–1721. Charles became king on the death of his father,
Charles XI, in 1697, when he was 15. Three years later the rulers
of Russia, Poland and Denmark formed an alliance to break
Sweden's command of the Baltic Sea, attacking Swedish-held
territories. Charles hit back with lightning speed and within a few
months he had invaded Denmark and forced the Danes to make
peace. He then defeated the Russians at Narva, on the Gulf of
Finland and invaded Poland. After a 6-year campaign he forced
the Polish king, Augustus, to give up the throne in favour of
Stanislas Lesczynski, an ally of Charles.

This settled, Charles invaded Russia but like NAPOLEON I and

Adolf Hitler in later years, he was defeated by the sheer size of Russia and its bitter winters. In 1709 his army was surrounded and captured at Poltava. Charles escaped to Turkey, where he remained in exile for 5 years while his late opponents proceeded to carve up the Swedish empire. Charles returned to Sweden in 1714, and renewed the war. In 1718 he invaded Norway, then under Danish rule, and was killed at the siege of Fredrickshald. Charles's military preoccupations left him with no time to consider marriage, and his sister Ulrica Eleanora succeeded him. Charles's brilliant campaigns earned him the nickname of the 'Swedish Meteor'.

CHARLES XIV (1763–1844) was a French soldier who became King of Sweden and founded the present Swedish royal house. He was born *Jean Bernadotte,* a lawyer's son, and he began his career as an ordinary soldier in the French army in 1780. Within 14 years he had become a brigadier-general. Under the republican government of France he held posts as minister of war, ambassador to the United States (though he never went there) and governor of Hanover. NAPOLEON I made him a marshal, and later gave him the title of Prince of Pontecorvo. His career as an army commander was chequered and he fell out of favour with Napoleon.

In 1809 the childless King Charles XIII of Sweden, whose advisers had admired Bernadotte's skilful governorship of Hanover, invited him to become his heir as crown prince of Sweden, under the name Charles John. Because the king was old and ill, Charles John at once took over the government as regent. In 1812 he joined Russia in a coalition against his former emperor, Napoleon, a move that brought about the union of Norway and Sweden. He led Sweden's armies against Denmark, then allied to Napoleon, and forced the Danes to cede Norway. In 1818 he became king on the death of Charles XII, and proved a popular and able ruler, though his autocratic ways provoked some opposition from time to time.

CH'IEN LUNG (1711–1799) was Emperor of China for 63 years. He was the fourth emperor of the Manchu (Ch'ing) dynasty, inheriting the throne from his father, Yung Cheng, in 1736. The Chinese empire was settled and large, and although there were several rebellions they were quickly and efficiently suppressed. Ch'ien Lung's forces also forced the ruler of Burma to pay tribute to China, and drove the Gurkhas of Nepal out of Tibet. The emperor agreed to a British appeal for permission to trade at Canton, which represented a considerable improvement in east-west relations at that time.

Ch'ien Lung is chiefly remembered for his devotion to the arts. He was an expert on painting, and a poet of considerable talent. His greatest undertaking was to try to assemble a library containing all the important books ever written in Chinese. This library ran to almost 36,000 volumes, and 7 copies were made of it, each one hand-written. At the same time he had hundreds of what he considered seditious books burned, and those who wrote them were executed. In 1796, Ch'ien Lung abdicated in favour of his son, Chia Ch'ing, but continued to hold the reins of power until his death 3 years later.

CNUT (995–1035), also known as *Canute*, was King of Denmark, Norway and England. Cnut inherited the throne of Denmark in 1014 from his father, Sweyn Forkbeard. Sweyn had already conquered England in a 3-year campaign, and driven out its Saxon ruler, Ethelred II (the Redeless or Unready). When Sweyn died the English invited Ethelred to return. Cnut led an army into England in 1015, and received immediate support from part of the country. When Ethelred died in 1016, Cnut and Ethelred's son, Edmund Ironside, divided the country between them. Edmund died the same year and Cnut became the sole ruler of England. In 1018 he also became sole ruler of Denmark, whose throne he shared with his brother Harald. He strengthened his position further by marrying Ethelred's widow, Emma of Normandy.

Having eliminated some possible Saxon rivals to the English throne by a series of cold-blooded murders, Cnut proceeded to govern England wisely, and largely according to the established tradition of the Saxon kings. In a letter to his subjects, written during a visit to Rome, he said: 'I have vowed to God to lead a right life in all things, to rule justly and piously my realms and subjects, and to administer just judgment to all.' During his reign there was peace in the land, and England grew in prosperity. His basic common-sense is illustrated by the traditional story of him rebuking his courtiers for their excessive flattery. Seated on the beach, he ordered the waves to retreat. When they did not he pointed out that this showed he was just an ordinary man.

Cnut acquired the control of Norway, a vassal state of Denmark, in 1028. On his death Cnut left England to his illegitimate son, Harold Harefoot, and Denmark to his son by Emma, Hardicnut, with Norway becoming independent. These drunken and dissolute men did not live long and England returned to the rule of a Saxon king, Edward the Confessor, a brother of Edmund Ironside.

CONSTANTINE I, THE GREAT (*c.* 274–337), was the first Christian Emperor of Rome. His full name was *Flavius Valerius Aurelius Constantinus* and he was the son of Constantius I, Emperor of the Western Roman Empire. Constantius died in Britain in 306, and the troops there immediately hailed Constantine as Augustus (emperor). There were several rival claimants to the imperial throne, leading to a good deal of fighting and bloodshed. In spite of this Constantine continued to rule Gaul and Britain, and in 312 he invaded Italy and defeated the Emperor Maxentius, who was the ruler in Italy, at the battle of the Milvian Bridge. Constantine adopted the Christian cross as a battle symbol, and soon after gaining power in Rome he introduced religious toleration, which helped the Christians greatly.

Constantine ruled as Emperor of the West until 324, when he fought and defeated the Emperor of the East, Licinius. Constantine then reunited the 2 halves of the Roman Empire under his sole rule. He decided to move his capital away from Rome, with its pagan traditions, and began the construction of a new city on the site of the little town of Byzantium. He dedicated the new capital, under the name of Constantinople, in 330. Its name has since changed to Istanbul.

In 325, he called the first world-wide council of the Christian Church, held at Nicaea (now the village of Iznik, in Turkey). Under his leadership the council adopted a creed that Christ was of the same substance as God. Constantine's piety grew as he became older. He built Christian churches, destroyed pagan temples, and showed favour to Christians, who had hitherto been persecuted. He was himself baptised as a Christian towards the end of his life. Though his firm, dictatorial reign brought peace to the empire for a while, his greatest work was the establishment of the Christian Church as a powerful, well-organised body instead of a small and persecuted sect. On Constantine's death the empire was divided among his 3 sons, Constantine II, Constantius II, and Constans. Civil wars followed, in which Constantine and Constans were killed, leaving Constantius as ruler of a united empire once more.

CYRUS II, THE GREAT (died 529 BC), founded the Persian Empire. He was the son of Cambyses I, King of Anshan, a province near the Persian Gulf that acknowledged the kings of the Medes as their overlords. According to legend Cyrus's mother was Mandane, the daughter of King Astyages of Media. Cyrus became King of Anshan in 559 BC. Some 6 years later he rebelled against Astyages and made himself master of Media. He spent several years crushing resistance and subduing the various small kingdoms that were allied to Media. He conquered Lydia and killed its king, Croesus, in 547 BC.

During the next few years Cyrus established himself as master of western Asia. He conquered Babylon in 539 BC. There he discovered large numbers of Jews who had been carried into exile by the Babylonians. In 536 BC Cyrus allowed the Jews to return to their homeland, and more than 42,000 did so.

As Cyrus was a master of the art of propaganda, it is sometimes difficult to tell which is the true account of an event and which the account that Cyrus wanted people to believe. His rebellion against Astyages is justified by the Median ruler's tyranny, and he is described as being welcomed by the Babylonians because of the 'evil rule' of their king, Nabonidus. The truth is probably close to these accounts, if not identical. What is certain is that Cyrus created a huge empire, stretching from the river Indus in Pakistan to the Mediterranean Sea, and that he ruled it well. He was killed in battle while trying to extend his empire still further to the east.

DARIUS I (*c.* 558 BC–486 BC), known as the Great, was one of the greatest of Persian rulers. He was a member of the Achaemenid royal family of Persia, but not closely connected to the reigning king, Cambyses, son of Cyrus I. A power struggle followed the death of Cambyses in 521 BC, in which Darius quickly emerged the victor and made himself king. A series of revolts against him flared in the next few years, but Darius was able to suppress them one by one, and by 518 BC he was master of the land.

He spent some time reorganising his large and unwieldy empire into provinces, each ruled by a satrap (governor). He improved the tax system, and with the aid of good roads and swift messengers kept in touch with all parts of his empire. He introduced Zoroastrianism as the official religion, though he respected the religions practised in the various provinces. His empire ranged from Egypt to west of the river Indus in present-day Pakistan, and extended into south-eastern Europe. But his campaign to subdue the Greeks ended in disaster at the battle of Marathon in 490 BC, and Darius died before a further attack on Greece could be mounted.

DAVID (*c.* 1040 BC–971 BC) was the second king to rule over all Israel. He was born at Bethlehem, the son of Jesse, a Judean farmer. He spent his early life looking after his father's sheep, while developing his considerable musical talents. His bravery in slaying wild animals that threatened his flock, and in the border warfare of the time, brought him to the attention of Saul, King of Israel, who gave him a post at his court. According to one tradition David killed Goliath, a gigantic champion of the Philistines, in single combat during one of the many wars of the time. He became head of the royal guard, and a close friend of Saul's son, Jonathan.

David was a popular hero of the time, which aroused Saul's jealousy. Warned in time, David fled to the hills, where he led a band of outlaws for some years. To avoid open warfare against Saul he eventually took service with Achish, the Philistine King of Gath. He was living at Ziklag, near Gaza, when news came that Saul and Jonathan had both died in a battle with the Philistines. David, after negotiations with the leaders of Judah, was acclaimed king of that country, a small part of southern Palestine. All Israel west of Jordan was in the hands of the Philistines, and the rest was under the weak rule of Saul's youngest son, Ishbaal.

After 7 years as ruler of Judah, David won Ishbaal's principal supporter, Abner, over to his side. Shortly afterwards Ishbaal was assassinated, and the leaders of Israel turned to David as the only man who could lead them. He was anointed King of Israel in 1006 BC.

The Philistines tried to crush the new king, but David defeated them decisively in two campaigns. He needed a strong and easily defended capital for his new kingdom, and found one at Jerusalem, which was occupied by the Jebusites. This apparently impregnable fortress fell when David sent his men in to capture it through a water tunnel which led in from outside the city walls. David also fought a series of wars against neighbouring kingdoms, thus making Israel's borders secure.

A long period of peace followed, during which David set up a strong central government. The seeds of future trouble were sown by David's private life. He set up a harem, with wives from many nations and sons by them who quarrelled among themselves. These family quarrels came to a head in the last years of David's life when his third son, Absalom, led a rebellion. In the campaign that followed Absalom was killed, to David's lasting grief. Soon afterwards David died, at the age of about 70. On his deathbed he arranged for his youngest son, SOLOMON, to be anointed as his successor.

In addition to his talents as a musician, David was a poet, and undoubtedly the author of some of the songs in the biblical *Book of Psalms*. Their beauty and religious sincerity added to the mystique that surrounded the name of David even in his own lifetime.

EDWARD III (1312–1377), King of England from 1327, embroiled his country in a conflict with France that dragged on until 1453, known to later generations as the Hundred Years' War. Edward's father, the worthless and morally corrupt Edward II, was deposed and murdered in 1327, and his 15-year-old son was proclaimed king in his stead. Edward III's mother, Queen Isabella, and her friend Roger Mortimer ruled in his name for 4 years, until Edward suddenly siezed power one night and had Mortimer executed.

Edward was a dashing and adventurous young man and fond of war; he quickly embarked on a campaign against the Scots, who had won their independence from English rule in his father's reign. Yet despite a victory at Halidon Hill in 1333 Edward was unable to make a secure conquest, and the Scottish king, David II, was able to return to the throne a few years later. In 1328 Edward openly claimed the throne of France, basing his claim on the rights of his mother, who was the sister of the French king, Charles IV (died 1328). The French, however, preferred Charles's cousin, Philip of Valois. Edward assumed the title of King of France in 1340, and tried unsuccessfully to invade France with an army, though he did win a great naval victory at the battle of Sluys. After another abortive campaign in 1342, he landed again in France in 1346 and won a resounding victory at Crécy. Yet the only real conquest of this campaign was Calais, which Edward colonised.

The final campaign in Edward's lifetime was conducted by his son, Edward, known as 'the Black Prince' from the colour of the armour he is said to have worn. The Black Prince captured the French king, John II, at the battle of Poitiers in 1356, fierce French resistance meaning that the best Edward could do was abandon his claim to the French throne in exchange for the province of Aquitaine, which he held for only a few years.

Edward's rule at home was just, though his wars cost the country a great deal. His court was brilliant. Edward's ideals of chivalry led him to found the Order of the Garter. In his later years his mental vigour declined, and he fell under the influence of his mistress, Alice Perrers. The Black Prince predeceased him and when Edward died he was succeeded by his grandson, Richard II, a boy of 10. More important than any other events of Edward's reign were the emergence of English instead of French as the language of law and parliament, and the growing independence of the House of Commons.

ELIZABETH I (1533–1603) became Queen of England at a time of religious and political turmoil. For 45 years she ruled her country by strength of will and brilliant statesmanship, leaving it stronger than it had ever been. Elizabeth was the daughter of HENRY VIII by his second wife, Anne Boleyn. When Anne was executed for treason in 1536 Elizabeth was declared illegitimate, but Henry was fond of her, and she was declared third in succession to the throne in 1544. Henry had her well educated, and she grew up a considerable scholar, master of Latin, Greek, French and Italian, and a talented musician.

During the brief reigns of her half-brother, Edward VI, and half-sister, Mary I, Elizabeth was several times suspected of conspiracy. These were dangerous times, when people could be executed on the flimsiest grounds. Under Edward England had become more Protestant, while Mary, a staunch Roman Catholic, had tried to convert the country back to her own faith. Elizabeth cleverly kept clear of all entanglements, and finally became queen when Mary died in 1558. Elizabeth had one advantage: the good-will of her subjects, sickened by the persecutions and burnings of Mary's reign. Gradually she reasserted the supremacy of the Protestant faith, and though there were continual Roman Catholic plots against Elizabeth, the main body of the English was firmly on her side.

Mary had made a disastrous marriage, to PHILIP II of Spain. Warned by this, Elizabeth prudently decided not to marry, and kept this resolve even though her ministers implored her to wed and provide an heir to the throne. Elizabeth was too dominant a personality to wish for a husband who might try to dominate her. Several European princes sought her hand, but she realised that the political problems involved would be too great for England's well-being. None of her own subjects was suitable, though she did for a while seem to encourage the advances of Robert Dudley, Earl of Leicester.

Another example of the dangers of an unsuccessful marriage was provided by her cousin, MARY, QUEEN OF SCOTS. Mary was Elizabeth's nearest heir, but she was a Roman Catholic which made her unacceptable to most of the English. When Mary had to flee from Scotland Elizabeth welcomed her, but kept her in close custody. Mary was the focus of Roman Catholic hopes in England, but was not openly involved in any of the many plots against Elizabeth until 1586. Reluctantly, then, Elizabeth agreed with her ministers that for her own and England's safety, Mary must die. Mary was found guilty of treason, and Elizabeth signed the death-warrant. This act solved the succession problem as the heir was now Mary's son, JAMES VI of Scotland, a staunch Protestant. Mary's death, however, did not end the religious problems, which had become international.

For several years England had been in a state of 'cold war' with Spain, its nearest rival for the wealth of the Americas. By diplomacy Elizabeth avoided open conflict for many years, but in 1588 Philip II, who regarded himself as the champion of Roman Catholicism, sent a Great Armada to fight against England. An English fleet, helped by bad weather, defeated the Spaniards in the English Channel. In an address to her troops at this time Elizabeth said: 'I know I have the body of a weak and feeble woman, but I have the heart and stomach of a king, and of a king of England too, and think foul scorn that Parma or Spain, or any prince of Europe should dare to invade the borders of my realm.' This sums up Elizabeth's love of her country and her great courage. Judiciously she kept England out of any disastrous and costly campaigns in the long war with Spain that followed, realising that she did not have the means to wage all-out warfare.

Through all adversities Elizabeth contrived to inspire great loyalty among her subjects, even while they complained about her penny-pinching ways when it came to raising an army or a navy. She was fortunate in the ministers she had, particularly William Cecil, Lord Burghley, her chief minister, and his son Robert, who succeeded him. She was also lucky to have warriors and explorers who furthered England's interests overseas, such as Sir Francis Drake, Sir Walter Ralegh, Sir Humphrey Gilbert, Sir Martin Frobisher, and Sir John Hawkins. The great literary figures of the Elizabethan Age included Edmund Spenser, Christopher Marlowe and William Shakespeare.

In her old age Elizabeth was attracted to a young courtier, the Earl of Essex. But by then she had lost the power to inspire men's loyalty, and Essex allowed himself to be caught up in a plot to overthrow Elizabeth's ministers. Elizabeth agreed to his execution in 1601, an act which threw a sadness over the last years of her life.

ELIZABETH II (born 1926) became Queen of the United Kingdom and Head of the Commonwealth when her father,

George VI, died suddenly in 1952. When Elizabeth was born her father, then Duke of York, seemed unlikely to inherit the throne. In 1936 Elizabeth's grandfather, George V, died, to be succeeded by her uncle, Edward VIII. Only a few months after becoming king, Edward abdicated in order to marry an American divorcee who was not acceptable as a queen, due to her status, and George VI succeeded him.

Elizabeth had a much less secluded upbringing than earlier members of the British royal family. She owed this to her mother, who before her marriage to the Duke of York was Lady Elizabeth Bowes-Lyon. This marriage was a break in the British tradition that royalty could marry only royalty. During World War II Elizabeth spent several months training with the Auxiliary Territorial Service, the women's branch of the British army. Two years later, in 1947, she married a distant cousin, Lieutenant Philip Mountbatten of the British Royal Navy. Philip was a member of the Greek royal family, though he was largely of Danish descent and had been brought up in England. He was given the title of Duke of Edinburgh.

George VI died while Elizabeth and Philip were on an official visit to Kenya, then a British colony. Official visits to Commonwealth and other countries were to occupy a large part of her time as queen. During her reign most of Britain's remaining colonies achieved independence, but as Head of the Commonwealth she acted as a link for these diverse peoples. In Britain itself her great contribution was to set an example of a happy and informal home life, while slowly but steadily trying to make the monarchy more democratic and less remote.

FERDINAND II OF ARAGON (1452–1516) was largely responsible for the unification of Spain, and making that country one of the most powerful in Europe. He was the son of John II of Aragon. At the time he was born Spain consisted of several small kingdoms, of which Castile was the most important. In 1469 Ferdinand married ISABELLA, half-sister of the King of Castile,

Henry IV. When Henry died in 1474 Isabella and Ferdinand succeeded as joint rulers of Castile. Five years later John's death gave
Ferdinand the throne of Aragon, which he later agreed to share
with Isabella. This put virtually all of Spain under one rule, except for the little kingdom of Navarre in the north and the Moorish
emirate of Granada in the south.

Ferdinand and his wife were known as the *Reyes Católicos*
(Catholic Kings). They were convinced and bigoted Christians,
and under their rule the Inquisition was established in Spain, with
the object of suppressing heresy and in particular of harassing the
Jews. The main target of the inquisitors was the group of Jews
known as Marranos, who were professedly converted Christians
but secretly followed their old religion.

The year 1492 was an eventful one for Ferdinand and Spain. In
that year Granada was wrested from the Moors; 200,000 Jews
were expelled from Spain, exile meaning death for many of
them; and Christopher Columbus sailed westwards under the
Spanish flag to the Indies and stumbled across the American
continent.

Ferdinand's armies conquered Naples, and scored many victories in northern Africa. The contemporary Italian statesman
Niccoló Machiavelli seems to have thought of these campaigns
as 'window dressing', to distract the attention of the Spanish
nobles so that they did not see how much power he was acquiring
over them. Ferdinand was an astute diplomat, and was anxious to
strengthen his position by marrying his children off advan-
tageously.

When Isabella died in 1504 her daughter Joan the Mad became
the nominal ruler of Castile, jointly with her husband, Archduke
Philip of Austria. But Philip died soon after, and Joan had to be
kept in confinement, so Ferdinand retained control of Castile
until his death. He was succeeded by Charles, son of Philip and
Joan, a member of the Habsburg family who later became
Emperor CHARLES V of the Holy Roman Empire.

FREDERICK I, BARBAROSSA (*c.* 1123–1190), was the great hero-king of German history. A handsome man with golden hair and the red beard that gave him the nickname of *Barbarossa*, he combined noble ideals with great personal ambition. He was the son of Frederick of Hohenstaufen, Duke of Swabia, whom he succeeded in 1147. Five years later he inherited the throne of Germany from his uncle, who advised the German princes to choose Frederick rather than his own son. Three years later Frederick was crowned as emperor; he was the first of the German rulers to adopt the title of *Holy Roman Emperor*.

Frederick's first task was to strengthen his position in Germany; to achieve this he placated or beat down all opposition. But for 30 years he was engaged in a struggle to bring Italy under his rule. The northern part was indeed part of the empire, but the city-states were inclined to rebel against their overlord. During his first campaign (1154–5) Frederick was crowned in Rome. In the second, in 1158, he subdued a rebellion in Mantua. Then Pope Adrian IV, with whom he was on friendly terms, died. Frederick backed Victor IV, one of the 2 claimants to the papacy, but Victor is generally regarded as an antipope—one not properly chosen. His rival, Alexander III, promptly excommunicated Frederick. When Victor died Frederick had another nominee, Paschal III, chosen as pope. Then in 1166 he descended on Italy again, determined to settle the papal question for good. His army stormed Rome, and he watched triumphant while Paschal was duly enthroned. Then plague broke out, and many of the soldiers died. Frederick had to retreat to Germany, leaving the Italian states in a rebellious mood. Not till 1174 was he able to return to the attack, then suffering a severe military defeat. But this led to peace between himself and the rightful pope, Alexander.

For the next few years Frederick was busy asserting his authority in Germany. His main rival was Henry the Lion, Duke of Saxony and Bavaria. Frederick defeated Henry in 1180 and sent him into exile. Three years later he agreed to a final settlement in Italy, which effectively gave the Italian states their independence.

What further action Frederick might have taken is uncertain, because the capture of Jerusalem by the Saracens (Arabs) in 1187 refocused the attention of many European leaders and aroused them to a crusade.

This was the third crusade launched to win the Holy Land back to Christianity. Frederick immediately assumed the leadership, traditionally the role of the emperor, and set out at the head of a large and magnificent army in 1189. The following year, while leading his troops across a small river in Asia Minor (Turkey), he was drowned. Legend has it that he sleeps in a cavern near Berchtesgaden, in southern Germany, surrounded by his knights, waiting for the call to wake and lead his people back to a golden age of power and prosperity.

FREDERICK II, THE GREAT (1712–1786), was King of Prussia. He was one of the leading soldiers of his age and also a fine musician. His father, Frederick William I, had him trained as a soldier, but Frederick preferred to read philosophy, study the flute and avoid his military duties. In 1730 he tried to escape to England, but was captured and court-martialled. His father made him watch the execution of a fellow-officer who had helped him, and was with difficulty persuaded not to have Frederick executed too.

Frederick spent the next 10 years studying military matters to please his father and studying French and political theory to please himself. When he finally succeeded to the throne in 1740 he introduced a totally new régime in Prussian life: it included the employment of Carl Philip Emmanuel Bach and Johann Quantz as court composers, the building of an opera house, and correspondence with such philosophers as Voltaire.

But Frederick was politically minded and knew the value of the fine army he had inherited. The death of the Holy Roman Emperor, Charles VI, led to a dispute over the succession, and Frederick at once seized his chance. While the empire was in confusion he invaded Silesia (now mostly part of Poland) and forced Charles's daughter, the Empress MARIA THERESA of Austria, to yield it to him. A further campaign in 1744-5 confirmed Frederick's possession of Silesia and peace followed which lasted for more than 10 years.

Although he hoped for peace to continue Frederick built up his armies and accumulated cash to fund a campaign if necessary. Meanwhile Austria made a secret pact with Russia, which included a plan to regain Silesia. Austria also signed a pact with France. In 1756 war broke out between Britain and France; Frederick, realising that France, Austria and Russia would be much too busy to attack him just yet, decided to attack first. By invading the neighbouring state of Saxony, he began what is known as the Seven Years' War. During a series of campaigns Frederick fought off attacks by Swedish, Austrian, Russian and French armies. Frederick was getting pretty near defeat when an unexpected event saved him: the empress Elizabeth of Russia died, and her successor, Peter III, was happy to make peace.

Frederick spent the next years restoring his country's economy, devastated by war. He also reformed the legal system of his country, developed a more efficient government and was widely respected as a military genius. When Austria and Russia decided to seize territory from the weak kingdom of Poland, Frederick shared in the plunder, gaining West Prussia. However, his government was based on his personal power and prestige, and when he died Prussia soon lost its power. Within 20 years it was crushed by the armies of NAPOLEON I.

GENGHIS KHAN (*c.* 1162-1227) was a tribal leader from Mongolia who made himself master of a vast empire, which ran right through central Asia from the Pacific Ocean to the river Dnieper in the west. His given name was *Temujin*, which meant 'The Finest Steel'. He was only 13 when his father died, and he spent the next few years hiding from his enemies, building up his military strength and gradually making himself a power in Mongolia. It was a time of ruthless warfare, and diplomacy that ensured support for Temujin from those who did not oppose him.

In 1206 Temujin held a council of the *khans*, the tribal princes: it gave him a new name, *Genghis Khan*, 'ruler of all men'. This event also marked an important step for the Mongol tribesmen: for the first time they were united under a strong leader and a code of laws, the *Yassa*, founded on tribal custom. It involved the punishment by death for such crimes as horse stealing, spying, and sorcery, but allowed freedom of religion such as no other laws did. Christians, Buddhists, Muslims, and many others were all welcome at Genghis Khan's motley court.

But though he had tamed his fierce tribesmen and ruled them with a rod of iron, Genghis Khan realised that he must keep them busy or there would be trouble. Accordingly Genghis embarked on a campaign of conquest. His first target was northern China, just south of the Mongol empire. This region was the empire of the Chins, who gave their name to China. By 1215 his armies had stormed Peking. At this point Genghis Khan turned westwards, where 2 other powerful kingdoms menaced his safety. They were Khorezm, a Muslim state that included Persia (Iran) and part of the Russian province of Turkestan, and the Kuman empire of southern Russia. Genghis himself led a campaign that lasted from 1219 to 1225, and took his victorious armies into Iran and Afghanistan, north of the Caspian Sea and onward to the Black Sea and what is now European Russia. It was a swift and bloody campaign, in which cities were destroyed and their people put to the sword.

Genghis then returned to his homeland. One last campaign lay ahead of him: to subdue the Chinese kingdom of Tangut, on the Yellow River. During this campaign Genghis grew sick and died, leaving to his third son, Ogatai, the greatest empire that had yet been seen.

See also KUBLAI KHAN.

GENSERIC (AD 395–477) was the king of the Vandals, one of the warlike German barbarian peoples who overran Europe during the Dark Ages. He is also known as *Gaiseric*. He succeeded his brother Gunderic as king in 428. At this time the Vandals, who had swept through Gaul, were settled in Spain. Genseric led them across the narrow Gibraltar strait into northern Africa, where he captured Carthage and made it his headquarters. From there his fleets terrorised the Mediterranean Sea as far east as the shores of Greece.

In 455 Eudoxia, the widow of the Roman emperor Valentinian, called on the Vandals to come to Rome to avenge the murder of her husband. The Vandals descended on the city in a large fleet. For 2 weeks they pillaged Rome, carrying off many works of art and doing such damage that their name has been synonymous with the destruction of beautiful things. When they finally sailed away from the ruined city Genseric took Eudoxia and her two daughters with him. The Romans later made 2 attempts to conquer Genseric, but he defeated both of them.

GEORGE III (1738–1820) was king of Great Britain for 60 years. During his long reign enormous changes swept his country. The early years of the Industrial Revolution transformed it from a purely agricultural state to one dominated by industry; the population doubled; Britain lost its colonies in North America and fought a long and bitter war against the French and NAPOLEON I.

George was the son of Frederick, Prince of Wales, who died in 1751. He became king in 1760 on the death of his grandfather, George II. A stupid and sometimes obstinate man, he was well aware of his great responsibilities and powers but had little idea how to make the best of them. He was a man of simple tastes, high moral values and patriotic feelings. He resolved to live up to his mother's command 'to be a King'.

He disliked the Whig Party who were in power when he came to the throne, his efforts to bring about a change of government leading to a series of short-lived ministries. In 1770 he found a politician with whom he could work—Lord North, a Tory. Though their policies at home were reasonable enough, George

and North were high-handed and tactless in their handling of the
13 colonies in North America. The king—supported by many of
his subjects—insisted that the colonies ought to pay the cost of
their own defence against the French, including part of the cost
of the Seven Years War, which ended in 1763. Efforts to tax the
colonists were clumsy and met with spirited opposition, which
George termed 'rebellion'. Soon there really was rebellion: the
13 colonies issued their Declaration of Independence, fighting a
war from 1776 to 1783 to make it good. Even when the war was
obviously lost the king felt it must be carried on as a matter of
principle.

In 1782 North resigned, but a year later George found a new
prime minister, William Pitt the Younger, whom he could trust.
George now spent less of his time in political matters, being
preoccupied with his family. He had many battles with his sons,
who did not share his simple tastes or moral standards, anxiety
driving him into a fit of insanity in 1788. He recovered the
following year but left the government more and more to Pitt.

A rebellion in Ireland by a group who wanted complete independence of their country from England broke out in 1799. It
was soon suppressed with the result that Pitt proposed that the
Irish parliament should be abolished and the two countries should
be completely amalgamated, under the title of the United Kingdom
of Great Britain and Ireland. This came about in 1801. In 1810,
after the death of his daughter Amelia, George's mind finally
gave way. Blind, bearded and raving, he spent his last years at
Windsor Castle under restraint, while his eldest son ruled as
Prince Regent.

GUSTAVUS I VASA (1496–1560) liberated Sweden from
Danish rule. Denmark, Norway, and Sweden had been united
under one sovereign since 1483, an alliance known as the *Union of
Kalmar*. The Swedes made several unsuccessful attempts to break
away, and under the leadership of the noble family of Sture
achieved semi-independence. Gustav Eriksson, another noble-

man, fought in the armies of Sten Sture the younger against the Danish kings, in 1517–18. But by 1520 the Danish king, Christian, had made himself master of all Sweden, murdering Gustav's father and two uncles among many other leading Swedes. Gustav then led a new rebellion which was successful, and in 1523 the Swedish nobility elected him as king. They later made the crown hereditary, so that Gustavus became the founder of a new dynasty, the House of Vasa.

Gustavus proved a just but hard monarch. He led Sweden in adopting the Protestant religion, but mainly as a political move. He acquired great wealth by confiscating Church lands, and used this to strengthen the power of the monarchy. In doing this he crushed opposition ruthlessly. When he died in 1560, after nearly 40 years as king, he left Sweden a strong, united country.

GUSTAVUS II ADOLPHUS (1594–1632) was a warrior king of Sweden, also noted for his reforms of government. He became king in 1611 on the death of his father, Charles IX. Neither Charles nor Gustavus had a cast-iron claim to the throne, and Gustavus had to strengthen his position by making concessions to the nobility and to the Riksdag (parliament). His real strength came from his choice of chief minister, Count Axel Oxenstierna. He helped to win over the nobility, and Gustavus's own tact and desire for reforms completed the victory.

When Gustavus became king, Sweden was at war with both Denmark and Russia although he quickly negotiated peace. However, a smouldering quarrel with Poland flared into open war in 1621. Sweden's king, Sigismund, was Gustavus's cousin and had been King of Sweden until Charles IX deposed him. The war lasted until 1629, when Gustavus made a peace treaty that gave him control of a number of Prussian ports. Although this war was not a part of the Thirty Years' War, which raged from 1618 to 1648, it effectively kept Poland from intervening in that dispute and also drew off support from the Holy Roman Emperor,

Ferdinand II, who was the leader of the Roman Catholic side in the Thirty Years' War.

In 1630 Gustavus decided he must intervene actively in the main conflict, supporting the cause of Protestantism. Strangely enough, he received financial support from the Roman Catholic Cardinal Richelieu, France's chief minister. Richelieu feared a victory by the emperor more than he wanted success for the Roman Catholic Church. Gustavus led an army of 30,000 men into Germany to relieve the siege of Magdeburg, a Protestant-held city. He failed, but soon after defeated the main Catholic armies under their commander, the Count of Tilly, in 2 bitter battles. Tilly was killed. In 1632 another great general, Albrecht von Wallenstein, led an army against Gustavus. In the battle of Lützen the Swedes were again victorious but Gustavus was killed.

He was succeeded by his daugher, Christina, with Oxenstierna as chief minister and effectively ruler. Oxenstierna was able to carry on Gustavus's policies.

HAAKON VII (1872–1957) was a Danish prince who was chosen to be King of Norway in 1905 when that country regained its independence from Sweden. Haakon was a younger son of Denmark's crown prince (later Frederick VIII). He was named Charles, and served in Denmark's navy. When he accepted the throne of Norway he adopted the name Haakon. He was chosen as king not only by Norway's parliament, the Storting, but by a plebiscite of the people. He proved a wise and tactful sovereign, and by the time the Germans invaded Norway in 1940 he had become deservedly popular. Haakon and his ministers escaped to England, where they kept the flag of Norwegian resistance flying during the dark years of World War II. In 1945 Haakon returned in triumph to Norway. He was succeeded by Olav V, his son by a British princess, Maud, daughter of Edward VII.

HADRIAN (AD 76–138) was the 14th emperor of Rome, and

one of the most capable. He came from a noble Roman family, and was named *Publius Aelius Hadrianus*. He was a distant cousin and the nearest relation of the Emperor Trajan, to whom he owed rapid promotion in the Roman army and administration. At the time of Trajan's death Hadrian was Roman prefect of Syria. The army acclaimed him as emperor in 117, his reign beginning with revolts in several parts of the empire. Hadrian dealt with some of these by curtailing the Roman frontiers in the east, where they extended beyond the river Euphrates.

In 121, having largely pacified the empire, Hadrian decided to tour it and see for himself the more remote provinces. He began by going westwards into Gaul (France), Germany and Britain. In Britain he left a lasting monument to his visit in the form of Hadrian's Wall, a 73 mile (117km) barrier across northern England to keep out the barbarian Picts and Scots. He visited most of the other outposts of the empire, where he strengthened fortifications and held parades and inspections to keep the troops stationed there up to the mark. He returned to Rome in 126 after an absence of more than 5 years. During this and his later travels the government went with him. This ensured the continuing power of the emperor and weakened the position of Rome itself as the hub of the empire.

In his later years Hadrian made a series of tours of the eastern part of the empire, reflecting the growing interest in the east among Romans of the time. The main result of all his journeyings was a considerable tightening up of the Roman bureaucracy, which had grown in a somewhat haphazard fashion. He also encouraged the construction of beautiful buildings; among the cities that benefited from his munificence were Rome, Athens, Ephesus and Smyrna. Perhaps his greatest failure was an attempt to found a Roman colony on the ruins of Jerusalem. The Jews, under the leadership of Simon Bar-Kochbar, staged a long and bloody revolt, which Hadrian suppressed only with difficulty.

Hadrian himself was a man of many interests and great culture —a poet, painter, musician, patron of all the arts and possessing an active and inquiring mind. His alternate bouts of meanness and generosity made him many enemies.

HAMMURABI (died 1686 BC) was the greatest king of Babylon. He became king in succession to his father, Sinmuballit, in 1728 BC: his long reign marked the beginning of the golden age of Babylon, which lasted for more than 1,500 years. Most of his reign was peaceful, though from time to time he waged brief and successful campaigns against neighbouring states and rebellious provinces. In the 39th year of his reign he conquered Assyria.

Hammurabi's fame rests on the great Code of Laws which he drew up: though based on older laws and customs, they were brought together and codified under his hand; his rigid enforcement of them brought both peace and justice to even the humblest citizen. Hammurabi took an active interest in the workings of the courts and ordered re-trials if he thought that justice had not been done. Many of the laws were harsh, punishments being on the principle of 'an eye for an eye'. A doctor who performed an unsuccessful operation lost his hand; so did a man who struck his father. If a house fell down and killed the owner, the architect was put to death. Hammurabi also fixed prices, set minimum wages and controlled the terms on which slaves were bought or hired.

His code was discovered engraved on a black stone block, buried in the ruins of the city of Susa in Iran. It ends with a comprehensive curse on anyone violating it.

HARUN AL-RASHID (766–809) was the most famous of the Caliphs of Baghdad. *Caliph* was the title borne by the heads of the Muslim community meaning *deputy*—deputy to Muhammad, the founder of Islam. Harun was a member of the Abbasid dynasty, which held the caliphate from 750 to about 1100. Harun's father was the Caliph al-Mahdi, who gave him military commands from the early age of 14. His successes earned him the title of 'al-Rashid', the 'rightly-guided', though this may have referred to the guidance of his guardian, Yaha, a member of the wealthy Persian family of Barmecide.

Harun succeeded his elder brother, al-Hadi, in 786. He continued his father's encouragement of scholarship and the arts, and made his court at Baghdad a centre of art and literature. The legends told in *The Thousand and One Nights* give a picture, though over-glamourised, of life at Harun's court. He ruled at first with the aid of Yaha and other members of the Barmecide family; he suddenly turned against them in 803 and had them imprisoned. The Barmecides had administered Harun's vast empire well, but it was cumbersome as well as large, meaning Harun had to quell a number of rebellions. War with the Byzantine empire raged from 791 onwards and was still going on when Harun died on his way to quash yet another revolt in the eastern part of his empire.

HENRY I (1068–1135), King of England, was the youngest son of WILLIAM THE CONQUEROR. He was nicknamed *Beauclerc* because he was a scholar, a rare thing for anyone outside the Church. Henry was born in England, 2 years after the Norman Conquest; his father left him no lands, only money. His eldest brother, Robert, was Duke of Normandy, his other brother, William Rufus, receiving the throne of England. William was considered to be a bad man and a bad king, and though Henry became one of his followers he was not blind to his brother's imperfections. One day in 1100 the brothers were out hunting when William was shot by Walter Tirel, one of his barons. It may have been an accident, but many historians think it was a plot masterminded by Henry. Within a few hours Henry had ridden to Winchester, seized the royal treasury there and persuaded the barons to acclaim him as king.

Robert, who had been absent on a crusade, tried to invade and claim the throne, but failed. Henry waited until 1106, then invaded Normandy and defeated Robert at the battle of Tinchebrai. Henry took Robert back to England and kept him prisoner till his death. Robert bore his captivity for 28 years until one day

Henry sent him a cloak that he had torn when putting it on. Robert, offended at receiving his brother's cast-offs, went on hunger-strike and died.

Henry was a good if stern ruler; he announced at his coronation that he would redress all wrongs done by his brother, also keeping his barons firmly in check. By accepting money payments from the barons instead of military service, he began creating a strong central government. Contemporary writers called him 'the lion of justice', and said: 'Good man he was, and there was great awe of him. In his days no man dared to harm another. He made peace for man and beast.' He also established a measure of control over the appointment of bishops, something the Church opposed bitterly.

Henry married twice. His first wife, Matilda, was a Scottish princess of Anglo-Saxon descent. By her he had several children, of whom 2 grew up: William, his heir, and a daughter, Matilda, also known as Maud. Henry pinned all his hopes for a strong England on his heir, but in 1120 William was drowned when his ship struck a rock on a voyage from France to England. Henry made his barons swear to support Matilda, but he knew their promises were mostly worthless, and he died a sad and disappointed man. His second marriage, to Adelais of Louvain, produced no children, but he had 20 illegitimate ones. In the event his nephew Stephen of Blois seized the throne and years of civil war followed.

HENRY II (1133–1189) founded the Plantagenet dynasty in England. He was the son of Matilda (Maud), daughter of HENRY I of England. Matilda's rightful claim to the throne was usurped by her cousin Stephen, Count of Blois. Stephen was 'a mild man, soft and good, and did no justice' according to contemporary chroniclers, and civil war raged between his supporters and those of Matilda. As a young man Henry made 2 attempts to drive Stephen off the throne, but failed ignominiously. In 1152 he married Eleanor, Duchess of Aquitaine, divorced wife of Louis

VII of France. Eleanor's dowry comprised a large part of France, so when Henry made his third landing in England in 1153 he came in strength. This time Stephen had to submit: he made Henry his heir. A year later Stephen died and Henry was king.

The new ruler was, like his grandfather, Henry I, a scholar. From his father, Geoffrey Plantagenet, Count of Anjou, he inherited a quick temper and great energy. He was a squat man, red-haired and freckled, with a harsh voice and brilliant eyes. He could remember every book he read and every face he saw—good qualities for a king. He began by curbing the barons, who had raided and plundered unchecked in Stephen's 18 years of misrule. He ordered them to pull down any castles they had built without permission; he reorganised the tax system and insisted that serious crimes should be tried only in the royal courts. The jury system came into general use during his reign. He chose wise counsellors to help him, among them Thomas Becket, a clever clerk who had taken Holy Orders as a deacon. Henry made Becket his chancellor or chief minister, the 2 men becoming firm friends. Becket was a shrewd politician and an even greater lover of pomp and good living than the king.

To reward him Henry made Becket Archbishop of Canterbury in 1162, hoping with his aid to increase the crown's control over the Church. But to his amazement Becket, who was ordained priest only the day before he became archbishop, took his new duties seriously. He resigned the chancellorship, strongly opposed any attempts by Henry to encroach on Church privileges, abandoned his fine clothes and good food, wore a coarse robe and lived only on vegetables and water.

In a proclamation known as the Constitutions of Clarendon Henry set out the rights of the crown over the Church as they had been in his grandfather's time. Becket refused to accept the constitutions, and when summoned to court to explain himself, fled into exile in France. After 6 years, peace was made between the 2 men and Becket returned to England, determined still to have his own way. His actions soon provoked Henry to wish, aloud, that somebody would rid him of 'this turbulent priest'. Four knights took him at his word and murdered Becket on the altar steps of Canterbury Cathedral. Henry, appalled, did penance for the crime, and it seemed for a time that Becket's death had defeated the king. But by the end of his reign Henry had largely got his own way with the Church.

Henry's later years were outwardly ones of power, but full of sorrow. He fell out with his wife, who left him to live in France. His three eldest sons, Henry (who died in 1183), Richard and Geoffrey, rebelled against him several times, urged on by their mother. Henry put up with their ingratitude, but when his favourite youngest son, John, joined a rebellion in 1188, he murmured 'Let things go as they will; I care no more', turned his face to the wall and died. He was succeeded by his eldest surviving son, the warrior-king, Richard Coeur-de-Lion.

HENRY V (1387–1422) became King of England in succession to his father, Henry IV, in 1413. He was an energetic, warlike young man, well read and fond of music. Though like all young men he liked a bit of fun, he was already taking a share of the government during his father's declining years, and when he ascended the throne he was ready to put frivolity behind him. His main ambition was to make himself king of France, reviving a claim long held by English kings. One beneficial effect of this outside interest was to secure greater unity in his own country, which was rife with plots in the first months of his reign.

In 1415 Henry invaded France with a carefully picked army of 10,000 men. He began by capturing Harfleur, at the mouth of the Seine; having lost thousands of men in dead, wounded and sick, he determined to march northwards towards the English-held port of Calais. Meeting with a greatly superior French army near the castle of Agincourt, Henry decided he must fight or perish. In a brilliantly fought battle he annihilated many of the French nobility and marched on to Calais in triumph. A long war followed, at the end of which Henry forced the French king, Charles VI, to acknowledge him as his heir and regent of France. He married Charles's daughter, Catherine, to make his position even safer. However, even in the hour of victory there was still much fighting to be done in France. During the next campaign he fell ill, probably with dysentery, and died. Charles died soon after, leaving Henry VI, baby son of Henry V and Catherine, to succeed to both thrones and a lifetime of wars and sadness.

HENRY VII (1457–1509) was the first English king of the House of Tudor, and one of the shrewdest politicians to sit on the English throne. His claim to the throne was slender. He made it through his mother, who was a great-granddaughter of John of Gaunt, Duke of Lancaster, third son of Edward III. His father was Edmund Tudor, Earl of Richmond, a Welsh squire whose mother, just to complicate matters, was Catherine of France, widow of HENRY V. He was also the last male member of the House of Lancaster whose long contest with the rival House of York brought about the destructive Wars of the Roses.

Henry actually won his crown by defeating and killing the Yorkist king, Richard III, in the battle of Bosworth Field in 1485. He then strengthened his position by persuading Parliament to acknowledge him, and by marrying Richard's niece, Elizabeth of York, daughter of Edward IV. Though this united the houses of York and Lancaster, it left a number of Yorkist claimants still alive and Henry spent a good deal of time crushing rebellions on behalf of one or another of them, twice on behalf of false claimants —Lambert Simnel, son of an Oxford joiner, and Perkin Warbeck, a Flemish servant.

One advantage of Henry's position was that the Wars of the Roses had involved the slaughter of a great many of the old nobility who might have claimed a share in the running of the country. This left Henry largely free to create a new nobility, drawn in many cases from the rising middle classes, all loyal to his interests. Recognising that wealth means power, Henry set himself to building up the royal fortunes. He levied heavy taxes, and kept a tight watch on expenditure—in particular he avoided the expense of war. Early in his reign he became involved in war with France as the ally of Spain and the Holy Roman Empire. He quickly made peace in exchange for payments from France. He also contrived to bring to an end the long-standing hostility between England and Scotland. His daughter, Margaret, was married to James IV of Scotland, an event that eventually brought the Stuarts on to the throne of England (see JAMES I and VI). He made an alliance with Spain, marrying off his elder son, Arthur, to Catherine of Aragon. When Arthur died a few months after, Catherine was betrothed to his brother, later HENRY VIII. Henry's final matrimonial coup was to try to marry his daughter Mary to Charles, Prince of Castile (later Emperor CHARLES V). After a 6 year betrothal the project fell through, Mary marrying Louis VII of France instead. She was widowed within the year.

Henry VII has been described as a shrewd businessman; he was also a crafty diplomat and the first English king to maintain permanent envoys abroad. From these men he received a constant stream of information on foreign affairs, enabling him to steer a successful course through the maelstrom of European politics. Allied to this he had a love of beauty and his chapel in Westminster Abbey is a lasting reminder of it.

HENRY VIII (1491–1547), the second Tudor king of England, is often thought of as a real-life Bluebeard—a fat, jovial man addicted to sport and good living. But underneath there was a cold, calculating monarch, much more like his father, HENRY VII.

As the younger son, Henry was trained for the Church, studying theology, languages, and music. He was a tall, handsome man, with long auburn hair, very athletic and an excellent sportsman. The death of his elder brother, Arthur, left him as heir to the throne and also betrothed to Arthur's widow, Catherine of Aragon, 6 years his senior. Lawyers having agreed that the marriage would be legal in the eyes of the Church, Henry made it one of the first acts of his reign, which began in 1509.

In his early years he appeared to leave the government to his ministers, in particular Thomas Wolsey, a butcher's son who had risen rapidly in the Church: but under the apparent indifference, Henry was watching events with a keen eye. When roused his temper was wicked, and he declared he would let no man govern him. Yet he had the ability to get on well with men of all classes, from servants to princes.

Unlike his father, Henry was eager to be involved in war, embarking on a campaign against France which brought several brilliant victories but no other real benefits. In 1520 Henry met the French king, Francis I, at a conference near Calais, known as the Field of the Cloth of Gold from the magnificence of both retinues. However, they failed to make friends and soon England and France were at war again. Once more the fight was expensive but inconclusive, and peace was restored.

By now Henry had a more serious problem: the succession. In that age a really strong personality was needed as head of state, and in effect dictator. Catherine had borne Henry 5 children, but only a daughter, Mary, lived. No woman had ruled England, and it seemed undesirable and unsafe to leave the throne to Mary. Henry was an intensely pious man, to whom Pope Leo X had given the title 'Defender of the Faith'. He wondered, seriously, whether his lack of children was a judgement for marrying his brother's widow. So he set Wolsey to negotiate with Pope Clement VII for a divorce. But the Holy Roman Emperor, nephew of Catherine, opposed the divorce, forcing the pope to say 'no'. Henry dismissed Wolsey, blaming him for the failure.

Henry now sought opinions from the universities of Europe as to whether his marriage was valid or not; their replies were favourable. The next step was an appeal to Parliament for support. The result was a series of Acts that declared the pope had no jurisdiction over the Church in England. Henry was declared head of the Church in England. Thomas Cranmer, the Archbishop of Canterbury, declared the king's marriage invalid, legalising a secret one to Anne Boleyn, a lady of the court. Though there was thus a definite break with Rome, Henry opposed more than a small move towards Protestantism, the Reformation at this time having little success in England. Many men opposed the king's actions, and were brutally put to death for their views.

Henry's new marriage was not a success. Anne gave birth to a daughter, the future ELIZABETH I, and then miscarried of a son. She was tempestuous and flighty, and Henry grew tired of her. She was accused of adultery and executed. Ten days later Henry married again, a docile girl named Jane Seymour. Jane produced the longed-for heir, later Edward VI, and died. Henry married 3 more times: first Anne of Cleves, a German princess whom he disliked at sight and divorced straight away; then another pretty lady of the court, Catherine Howard, who took a lover and was promptly executed for treason; and finally a tactful, quiet woman, Catherine Parr, already twice widowed, who looked after him till he died and then married a fourth husband.

A byproduct of Henry's break with Rome was the dissolution of the monasteries, which had enormous wealth. Some of this went to the Crown, some to reward Henry's supporters.

HENRY III (1551–1589) was the last French king of the House of Valois. He was the youngest of the 3 sons of Henry II who became kings of France, and all were more or less under the influence of their selfish, strong-willed mother, Catherine de Médicis. Henry combined religious fervour with immorality. He was an effeminate creature, surrounding himself with a group of like-minded courtiers known as his *mignons*. He was married but had no children.

Before Henry became king he held the title of Duc d'Anjou. With his mother he planned and helped to carry out the infamous Massacre of St Bartholomew's Day in 1572, when 10,000 Huguenots (Protestants) were butchered in Paris and other cities. The following year, as a result of great French diplomatic activity, Henry was offered the crown of Poland, as its king, Sigismund II, had died without an heir. Hardly had he arrived in Poland when his brother, Charles IX, died and Henry returned hastily to France as its king. The Poles elected Stefan Batory as king instead.

Under pressure, Henry made concessions to the Huguenots, but this provoked an alliance known as the Catholic League, led by Henry, Duc de Guise, to oppose the Huguenots. The Roman Catholics were the more alarmed because the Protestant leader, Henry, king of Navarre, was the heir to the French throne. A civil war broke out, known as the War of the Three Henrys. The Catholic League gained the ascendancy, whereupon Henry had Henry of Guise murdered, himself fleeing to the army of Henry of Navarre for protection. Eight months after, a fanatical friar stabbed Henry to death. He was succeeded by Henry of Navarre as HENRY IV.

HENRY IV (1553–1610) was one of the greatest of France's kings. He was the first member of the Bourbon dynasty on the French throne. The son of Antoine de Bourbon, duc de Vendôme, and Jeanne d'Albret, Queen of Navarre, he became King of Navarre on the death of his mother in 1572. Navarre was a shadowy kingdom on the borders of France and Spain, mostly Basque in population. The Spanish part had already been annexed by Castile, and Navarre finally ceased to exist not long after Henry's death.

Henry was brought up as a Protestant and had a distinguished military career in France's religious wars. In 1572 he was married to Margaret, sister of the French kings Francis II, Charles IX, and HENRY III. He was spared in the massacre of St Batholomew's Day 6 days later but was kept almost a prisoner at the French court and coerced into adopting the Roman Catholic faith. He escaped in 1576 and led a series of rebellions against Henry III. But in 1589 he succeeded to the French throne on Henry's death by assassination.

The new king had resumed his Protestantism and faced a long and stubborn war against the Roman Catholic League before he could claim that his throne was safe. Military victories coupled with compromise finally settled the matter: Henry once more accepted the Roman Catholic religion, saying cynically: 'Paris is well worth a Mass.' In 1598 he also made peace with the fiercely Catholic PHILIP II of Spain, who had been supporting Henry's enemies inside France.

At home, Henry pacified the Protestant section of the country by the Edict of Nantes, also in 1598. This gave Protestants equal political rights with the Roman Catholics, although it did not give them complete freedom of worship. Having secured peace, Henry set about repairing the damage done by years of civil war. In this he was ably aided by his chief minister, Maximilien de Béthune, Baron de Rosny, whom he later made Duc de Sully. Together Henry and Rosny built up the royal finances, paid off debts and asserted the authority of the crown over the barons.

To encourage trade, Henry had a system of canals dug, improved roads and negotiated commercial treaties with England and other countries. In foreign affairs he dealt himself a strong hand by establishing a well-organised and equipped army. He prepared a Grand Design, planned to ensure perpetual peace through the establishment of a general council of Europe under the chairmanship of the Holy Roman Emperor. This did not prevent him from preparing to go to war against the Emperor in order to ensure the Protestant succession in the little duchy of Jülich, which lay not far from Cologne. However, before he could lead his armies to battle he was assassinated by a crazy schoolmaster, François Ravaillac.

Henry's first marriage was childless, so he divorced Margaret in 1599 and married Marie de Médicis, a member of the powerful Italian Medici family. Their 6 children included Henry's successor, LOUIS XIII. Henry had many mistresses and was long remembered by the French as a great lover as well as being a great statesman.

HENRY I (*c.* 876–936), king of Germany, laid the foundations of the German empire, later to be known as the Holy Roman Empire. He succeeded his father as Duke of Saxony in 912 and spent the next few years waging war with the German king, Conrad I. When Conrad lay on his deathbed he named Henry, as obviously the strongest of the German princes, to be his successor. A meeting of the princes duly elected Henry as king in 919. Legend has it that he was out hunting when the news of his election was brought to him, and that henceforth he was known as *Henry the Fowler*.

Henry spent most of his reign fighting to keep his throne, beating off attacks from the Magyars of Hungary and subduing rival claimants for power. He left a strong centralised government to his son, OTTO I.

HENRY IV (1050–1106), King of Germany and Holy Roman Emperor, succeeded his father at the age of 6, and for many years Germany was ruled by his mother, Agnes, supported by leading members of the Church. By the time Henry took over the reins of power himself in 1066, a great deal of that power had passed into the hands of the Church. Henry began his reign by defeating a rebellion in Saxony and trying to win back lands lost during his mother's regency.

Trouble flared with the election of a new pope, Gregory VII, in 1075. Gregory declared that no lay person could make Church appointments or confirm grants of land. Since half the lands of Germany were in the hands of abbots and bishops, this would have left Henry almost powerless. Gregory accused Henry of misgovernment and vice, calling him to Rome to answer these charges. Henry, a vigorous, fiery person, retorted by calling a council and declaring Gregory deposed as pope. Gregory retorted by excommunicating Henry and in turn deposing him. At this point the Saxons rebelled again, and many of Henry's barons threatened to rebel also unless he submitted to the pope.

Submission was made as unpleasant as possible. Gregory was staying at the castle of Canossa, in north central Italy. It was winter; Gregory made Henry stand barefoot and huddled in a plain woollen gown in the snow outside the castle for 3 days before he would allow him in to kneel and sue for forgiveness. Peace, though bought at such a price, gave Henry time to deal with his rebellious subjects, who set up a rival king named Rudolf. Civil war raged for 3 years, at the end of which Henry emerged strong enough to breathe new threats against Gregory—who promptly excommunicated him again.

This time Henry was able to call a council of German and Italian churchmen, who declared Gregory deposed and elected an antipope, Clement III. In 1080 Henry marched into Italy, stormed Rome and had himself crowned as Emperor by Clement in 1084. Gregory's ally, Robert Guiscard, duke of Apulia, drove Henry out of Rome, and back to Germany, but in doing so he sacked Rome, committing such atrocities that Gregory had to leave the city: his friends had proved worse than his enemies. Gregory died in exile.

Henry spent the rest of his troubled reign in civil war. In 1093 his eldest son and heir, Conrad, rebelled against him; and after Conrad died the next son, Henry, also took up arms against his father. A new pope, Paschal II, excommunicated Henry IV once more. The younger Henry took his father prisoner by treachery, compelling him to abdicate. The unhappy emperor escaped, and was preparing a new onslaught with foreign aid when he died. His son succeeded him as Henry V, and carried on the struggle against the papacy with equal fury. Eventually emperor and pope reached a compromise in 1122.

HEROD THE GREAT (73 BC–4 BC) was King of Judaea when it was under Roman control. He was the son of Antipater, a wealthy and influential man from southern Palestine. As a young man Herod became friendly with the Roman leader Mark Antony and other Romans. As a result he became governor of the province of Galilee at the age of about 25. Mark Antony later promoted him to the position of tetrarch of Galilee. But in 40 BC civil war broke out and Herod had to flee for his life. He took refuge first at Masada, a fortress he had prepared near the Dead Sea, and then went to Rome. There he was appointed king over all Judaea and sent back to Palestine with an army to subdue his new kingdom. After a 2-year campaign he made himself master of Judaea in 37 BC.

Herod's position was difficult: by birth he was an Edomite, one of the partly Arab races. He had married Mariamne, a princess of the Hasmonean dynasty which had ruled Israel for almost 150 years, but the Hasmoneans regarded him as a usurper. The orthodox Jews distrusted him because of his allegiance to Rome and his willingness to build temples for the worship of Roman gods.

Herod's cold, cruel and calculating nature enabled him to overcome all his problems. He placated the Jews by respecting their religious beliefs and building for them a new temple in Jerusalem, part of which still survives as the Wailing Wall. He maintained order with the aid of an efficient spy system and bands of hired mercenaries. Any sign of rebellion Herod crushed with swift severity. He had nearly 50 leading Judaeans executed in the first years of his reign; and not even his uncle and his brother-in-law were safe from execution if they threatened his safety. Herod faced many plots against himself, especially from Mariamne's family. In 29 BC, suspecting Mariamne of infidelity as well as conspiracy, Herod had her murdered, together with her 2 sons, her mother and her grandfather, Hyrcanus the High Priest, a former king of Judaea. He repented of this crime.

In his later years Herod suffered from a painful disease which affected his mind. His suspicions grew and so did his cruelty. Not long before his death he had his eldest son, Antipater, killed and also ordered the slaughter of all the very young children of Bethlehem because of a prophecy that a future king of the Jews had been born there. He died in 4 BC. Altogether Herod had 10 wives and 14 children. He left his kingdom to be divided among his 3 remaining sons, a division to which the Roman emperor AUGUSTUS agreed. In spite of the welter of blood and violence that surrounded his last years, Herod was one of the most capable rulers in Palestine's history.

HUGH CAPET (*c.* 938–996), King of France, founded the Capetian dynasty which ruled France until 1328. He was the grandson of HENRY I (the Fowler) of Germany, duke of the Franks, and one of the most powerful of French nobles. On the death of Louis V, known as *Le Fainéant* or 'Do-nothing', who left no direct heir, the French barons decided that the crown should be a matter of election. Their choice fell on Hugh, who became king in 987. Hugh had comparatively little power over the French barons, and even the frontiers of his kingdom were not clearly defined. He devoted his time to staying out of trouble, refusing to become one of the princes of the Holy Roman Empire, and wooing his more difficult subjects with gifts of land.

The kingship would probably have been a matter of election after Hugh's death but for his foresight in having his son, Robert, crowned as king during his own lifetime, a process known as *co-optation*. Successive Capetians carried on the practice for 200 years until the dynasty was so firmly established that it was no longer necessary.

Hugh's nickname of *Capet* came from the cape he wore in his office as abbot of St Martin de Tours.

IBN SAUD (*c.* 1880–1953) founded the kingdom of Saudi Arabia, which takes its name from him. He came of a family of Arab tribal leaders; his father was sultan of Nedj, in central Arabia. This was one of the independent parts of Arabia, a great deal of it lying under Turkish rule. Ibn Saud began his career by reconquering Nedj from the rival Rashidi tribe. During World War I the British encouraged Arab revolts, but gave their support to Hussein of the Hijaz. Hussein was proclaimed king of the Arabs in 1916. Ibn Saud refused to acknowledge Hussein and began a campaign to overthrow him. By 1926 he was proclaimed king of the Hijaz and sultan of Nedj.

E

Ibn Saud established the capital of his new kingdom at Riyadh, changing the name of the country in 1932 to Saudi Arabia. During the next few years he concluded peace treaties with all the neighbouring states and with Britain, which had interests in the Persian Gulf. In 1933 he launched his country on the road to prosperity by allowing United States oilmen to exploit the country's enormous petroleum deposits.

His full Arabic name was *'Abd al-Aziz ibn 'Abd al-Rahman al-Faisal ibn-Saud.*

ISABELLA OF CASTILE (1451–1504) helped to unite Spain as one kingdom by her marriage in 1469 to FERDINAND II OF ARAGON. Isabella was the half-sister of King Henry IV of Castile, a weak and incompetent king said to have strange habits. Because the nobles of Castile suspected that Henry's daughter Joan was not in fact his own child, they compelled him to acknowledge Isabella as his heir. When Henry died in 1474 Isabella and Ferdinand became joint rulers of Castile, uniting nearly all Spain under their joint sovereignty when Ferdinand succeeded to the throne of Aragon in 1479.

Isabella was intensely religious and she played a leading part in the policy that led to the establishment of the Inquisition in Spain and the expulsion or execution of most of the country's Jews. The queen was an active sharer of power with her husband and was prepared to act on her own if necessary. It was she and not Ferdinand who listened to the plans of Christopher Columbus for a voyage westwards to the Indies, and she provided the money for the explorer's momentous voyage in 1492 which led to the discovery of America.

Of Isabella's 5 children 2, Isabella and Maria, became in turn the wives of Manuel I of Portugal; her only son predeceased her; Joan became the mother of CHARLES V, the Holy Roman Emperor, and was considered mad for most of her life; and Catherine married HENRY VIII of England.

IVAN III, THE GREAT (1440–1505), became Grand Prince of Muscovy (the region around Moscow) in 1462. He laid the foundations of the Russian Empire by expanding and strengthening his domains. In 1478 he annexed the city of Novgorod and the vast lands under its control. Two years later he defied the Tatars, who had claimed tribute from the Grand Princes of Muscovy for many years, and freed Muscovy from Tatar control. Gradually he brought all the small principalities of northern Russia under his rule, and controlled an empire that extended from the Polish border to east of the Ural Mountains. Ivan fought several campaigns in an effort to subdue Poland and Lithuania, but such gains as he made were only temporary.

In 1472 he married Sophia, niece and heir of the last Byzantine emperor, exiled when Constantinople came under Turkish rule in 1453. This marriage gave Ivan a claim to be considered as the natural successor of the Byzantine rulers, the last survivors of the old Roman Empire.

IVAN IV, THE TERRIBLE (1530–1584), the grandson of IVAN III, was the first *tsar* or emperor of all Russia. He adapted the title from the Latin word *Caesar*. Ivan succeeded his father, Vasily III, at the age of 3. During his minority the country was ruled by a Council of Boyars, the wealthy landlords of Russia. Ivan assumed power when he was 16, and was crowned as tsar the following year. He was already renowned for his viciousness and cruelty, but for some years these traits were kept in check by the influence of his wife, Anastasia, and his principal advisers, a priest named Sylvester, and a minor nobleman, Alexis Adashev. With their aid Ivan curbed the power of the boyars, and in 1552 captured the Volga river area of Kazan from the Tatars.

In 1560 Anastasia died and about the same time Ivan dismissed Sylvester and Adashev. Without their restraining influence his cruelty came more noticeable. He launched a personal reign of terror, in which princes, noblemen, and others were put to death, banished or ordered to become monks. He formed a bodyguard of secret police, the Oprichnina, whose members were chosen for their loyalty and cruelty. Led by the tsar, the Oprichniks murdered and tortured all who were suspected of treason—and they were many. In the late 1560s Ivan added a form of religious mania to his other signs of insanity.

In 1569 he launched a punitive expedition against the city of Novgorod, which he accused of rebellion. His private life was no better: he had altogether 7 wives, one at least dying under very suspicious circumstances. His eldest son, the Tsarevich Ivan, shared his taste for rape and murder; but one day father and son quarrelled, and Ivan struck his son and killed him. He spent his remaining years in alternate fits of remorse and deeds of violence, becoming a monk on his deathbed.

In spite of his bloodlust, Ivan showed many signs of wise statecraft. He developed diplomatic relations with other countries, particularly England, expanded his empire eastwards to take in Siberia and built up Russia's overseas trade.

JAMES I & VI (1566–1625) united the thrones of England and Scotland. He was the son of MARY, QUEEN OF SCOTS, by her second husband, Lord Darnley. He became King of Scots when he was just over a year old, on his mother's abdication. Until 1583 the government of Scotland was carried on by a succession of regents, while James received a thorough education, particularly in Protestant theology. He was a clever man but inclined to be self-opinionated and pedantic. When he began to rule in his own right he followed a policy of playing off the Roman Catholics and the Protestants against one another in order to get his own way. He believed sincerely in his own, God-given authority—'the divine right of kings'.

Because HENRY VIII's children, Mary, Edward VI and ELIZABETH I, all died childless, James became the next in line to the English throne, through his great-grandmother Margaret, daughter of HENRY VII. As he was a Protestant, Elizabeth and her ministers agreed that he should succeed her, and in 1603 he was proclaimed King of England. By comparison with Scotland, England was a rich country but James soon found that he was short of money. The value of money was falling but the royal revenues were not increasing to compensate. Those revenues had to cover not only the court expenses but all the expense of government. James clashed repeatedly with Parliament by trying to raise more money through extra taxes. He also faced religious problems: James believed in a Church with bishops, while a great many English Puritans were intent on simplifying religious practices. The policy of 'divide and rule' which had served James well in Scotland did not work in England; in particular he did not understand Parliament. The members of Parliament in turn did not understand James. They were accustomed to the Tudors and their autocratic ways. James, coming to them claiming divine right, long practice in the art of kingcraft and the right to lecture them on any occasion, might have carried things off better had he had the Tudor presence. But he was an awkward, undignified man, with a broad Scots accent they found hard to follow. In his later years he left the conduct of affairs to his favourites, first Robert Carr, Earl of Somerset, who was later mixed up in a murder scandal, and then George Villiers, Duke of Buckingham, who was arrogant, witty and reckless.

Two events of James's reign are still remembered. First was the Gunpowder Plot, a Roman Catholic conspiracy to blow up James and Parliament together. One of the conspirators, Guy Fawkes, a Yorkshire gentleman, was found in the cellars of Parliament surrounded by barrels of gunpowder. The other was a new version of the Bible, which was prepared by a panel of scholars instructed by James to produce an edition free from any religious bias. This was the Authorised Version, first printed in 1611. Its beautiful, poetic English has captured the minds of people ever since and is, despite the work of more modern scholars, still the most popular.

JUSTINIAN (483–565) was the last of the great Roman emperors. He came from a comparatively humble family and was born near Skopje, in present-day Yugoslavia. His uncle, Justin, a successful military leader, was elected Byzantine Emperor (that is, emperor of the Eastern Roman empire) in 518 and relied heavily on his clever nephew to help him rule. When Justin died Justinian succeeded him, adopting the name Justinian: his original name was *Petrus Sabbatius*.

Justinian set out to restore the glories of the Roman empire. In a series of campaigns he fought off, and then bought off, attacks from Persia in the east. He then turned his attention to the west, regaining many parts of the empire that had fallen under barbarian rule, including Italy, northern Africa and part of Spain. A devout Christian, he made war on heretics within the faith and also on Jews and pagans.

His greatest amd most lasting work was to set up two commissions to collect all the vast body of Roman law into one comprehensive code, the *Corpus Juris Civilis* (Body of Civil Law). This great work has formed the basis of the legal systems of many modern countries. It was in four parts: the *Codex*, or collection of laws; the *Digest*, a series of extracts from the works of Roman lawyers; the *Institutes*, a textbook of legal principles; and the *Novels*, new laws issued by Justinian.

KUBLAI KHAN (1216–1294), the greatest of the Mongol emperors, completed the Mongol conquest of China. He was the grandson of GENGHIS KHAN. Kublai's eldest brother, Mangu, was elected Great Khan in 1251. Mangu gave Kublai the eastern part of the already vast Mongol empire to administer. When Mangu died 9 years later the Mongol nobles elected Kublai to serve in his stead. Kublai had to contend with armed opposition from other descendants of Genghis Khan, including his own younger brother, but he defeated them and made himself absolute master of the Mongol empire.

In 1267 Kublai launched an all-out campaign to conquer the southern part of China, which was still independent. When he brought it to a successful conclusion in 1279 Kublai found himself master not only of China, but of an empire stretching from the Pacific Ocean in the east to southern Russia and part of Poland in the west: it included modern Iran, Afghanistan, and Korea, and most of Turkey, Burma and Vietnam. Parts of this empire were not under Kublai's direct rule, but acknowledged him as their overlord.

China was the most important part of Kublai's empire. It was there that he founded a new dynasty, the Yüan, which ruled until 1368. He also moved his capital from Karakorum (Black Walls), Mongolia's only city, to Chungtu, which he named Khanbalik, the 'City of the Khan'. Its name today is Peking. About 150 miles (250km) to the north Kublai built a magnificent summer palace at Shang-tu—the Xanadu of Samuel Taylor Coleridge's poem about Kublai Khan. There, and in Peking, Kublai lived in splendour; and it was there that the Venetian traveller Marco Polo came to see him, and stayed in his service for 24 years.

Kublai was a wise ruler and left a great deal of Chinese life unchanged. He kept a close watch on all parts of his vast domain, sending Marco Polo and others as his envoys to carry out his orders and to report on the situation. He was tolerant of religious faiths, he himself being a Buddhist. Polo's account of life at court tells us that the Great Khan held 13 grand banquets every year, at which up to 6,000 people were entertained with rich food, and drink served in golden cups.

Kublai's dynastic name in Chinese was Shih-tsu. He was succeeded by his grandson, Temur Oljaitu.

LOUIS XIII (1601–1643) became king of France at the age of 9 after the assassination of his father, HENRY IV. His mother, Marie de Médicis, was regent during Louis's boyhood. She was an obstinate woman, much influenced by her favourites, and ruled France unwisely in an atmosphere of plots and civil strife. In 1617 Louis had his mother's main favourite, the Marquis d'Ancre, assassinated, taking control of the realm himself. Three years earlier the States General of France had met—the last time before the French Revolution in the reign of LOUIS XVI.

Louis, though physically not strong, was very conscious of his royal powers and authority. Yet like his mother he spent most of his time under the influence of other people. He was fortunate that his chief adviser and minister from 1624 was the brilliant and wily Armand-Jean Duplessis, Cardinal Richelieu. Richelieu was an impoverished nobleman who became a priest in order to keep in his family the bishopric of Luçon. His rise was rapid, both in the Church—he was made a cardinal at the age of 37—and as a minister of the crown. Richelieu was vain, ambitious and as much a lover of pomp and wealth as any king: but he also loved France, and served it and its king well.

Among his first acts was the destruction of the power of the Huguenots, the French Protestants: they were left with only freedom of worship. Richelieu and Louis then set out to curb the power of the nobles, which had led the country into civil war on several occasions. Richelieu created a new system of government by civil servants, responsible to the central government in Paris. Local authority, which was often under the control of a local nobleman, was seriously weakened. The army was also firmly under the control of the crown.

Richelieu's foreign policy was devoted to keeping France strong and preventing other powers from acquiring too much strength. In the Thirty Years' War of 1618–1648, which began as a conflict between Protestants and Roman Catholics, Richelieu led Roman Catholic France into the conflict on the Protestant side, against the Habsburg family who dominated Germany and Spain. This happened although Louis was married to Anne of Austria, daughter of the Spanish king Philip III. By the time Richelieu died, a year before his master, he had made Louis XIII a power in Europe and an absolute monarch. Louis and Anne did not have any children until they had been married 23 years, so when Louis died he was succeeded by a boy of 5, Louis XIV.

LOUIS XIV (1638–1715) ruled France for 72 years, the longest reign of any European monarch. He succeeded his father, Louis

XIII, in 1643, when he was 5 years old, his mother, Anne of Austria, acting as regent. To help her she had Jules, Cardinal Mazarin, who had succeeded Cardinal Richelieu as France's chief minister in the last year of Louis XIII's reign. Mazarin was not always popular but his administration was generally sound. He helped to bring about the peace that ended the Thirty Years' War in 1648. At that time an insurrection broke out in France: it was a revolt by a group known as the *Fronde*, who opposed the central government set up in the previous reign. It was quelled by 1653. Mazarin died in 1661, and Louis, now 24 years old, became his own chief minister.

Louis ruled with a small council of state, an autocrat who would stand no opposition. He once said '*L'état, c'est moi*' (I am the state), and it was a true statement. His court was magnificent, the envy and example of all Europe. Louis encouraged painters, writers, philosophers and musicians. He himself was fond of dancing and he was often known as *the Sun King* from a rôle he had danced in a court ballet. He built a new palace for himself at Versailles, away from the smells and the people of Paris, where he entertained in a style that gave him another of his nicknames, *The Grand Monarch*. The king had several mistresses but he was far too shrewd to allow them to influence his political judgement. Louis was married as a boy to Marie Thérèse of Austria, by whom he had 6 children; they all predeceased him. After the queen died he secretly married one of his mistresses, the Marquise de Maintenon.

It was about this time that Louis began an intensive persecution of the Huguenots (Protestants). Deprived of many of their rights as citizens, and of the freedom to worship as they pleased, about 400,000 Huguenots fled the country. They included many skilled workers; two of the places they went to, the Netherlands, and Brandenburg, in Germany, developed their industries as a direct result of the Huguenot immigration.

In foreign affairs Louis fought 4 wars. In the first, in 1667–68, he won some territory in the Netherlands from its Spanish rulers. In the second he secured more territories in the Netherlands and also some from the German states bordering France. When this war ended in 1684 Louis was at the height of his power, both in France and in Europe. The third war, in 1689–97, was designed to claim the German state of the Palatinate for his sister-in-law, the Duchess of Orléans. After some successes and some defeats, all France gained was the province of Alsace and the city of Strasbourg. The last war, the War of the Spanish Succession (1701–14), Louis fought to establish the right of his grandson, Philip V, to succeed as King of Spain. This war ranged the Dutch, the English and most of the Holy Roman Empire against France. France suffered a series of defeats, losing possessions in North America to England and some border towns to the Netherlands when peace was made. But the worst losses were in finance and reputation; when Louis died a year later it was in an atmosphere of gloom.

Louis's eldest son and grandson both predeceased him, the throne passing once more to a minor, his great-grandson LOUIS XV.

LOUIS XV (1710–1774) came to the throne of France as a boy of 5, succeeding his great-grandfather, LOUIS XIV. The duc d' Orléans, a nephew of Louis XIV, was appointed regent. The kingdom was bankrupt; the nobility were wealthy; but the poorest people, crippled by taxes, were very poor indeed. The duke was succeeded in 1723 by the duc de Bourbon, a distant relative of the king. Bourbon increased taxes, making matters worse. But he was ousted in 1726 by Cardinal André de Fleury, Louis's tutor, a man of real ability. Although France intervened in the War of the Polish Succession (1733–35), gaining Lorraine by it, the years until 1740 were peaceful and the shaky French finances improved greatly.

In 1740 France became involved in the War of the Austrian Succession, in which France joined with Prussia and other powers in trying to prevent the Empress MARIA THERESA succeeding as ruler of Austria. France gained nothing from this conflict, which involved it mostly in war with Britain. In 1743 Fleury died and

Louis assumed the rôle of chief minister himself. Unfortunately he was weak, and sought refuge from the affairs of state too often in pleasure. His mistresses, notably the Marquise de Pompadour, influenced him considerably and the court became a morass of petty intrigues and quarrels.

Disaster came with the Seven Years' War (1756–63), in which Britain was France's chief opponent. By the time it ended France had lost its colonies in India and Canada, and the nation's finances were as they were before Fleury's improvements. When Louis died the power of the monarchy was declining. The extravagance of the court and the poverty of the country were already fermenting unrest, which was to come to a head in the reign of Louis's grandson and successor, LOUIS XVI.

LOUIS XVI (1754–1793) succeeded his grandfather, LOUIS XV, in 1774. Aged 20, he was the first French king since HENRY IV to come to the throne old enough to rule. He was already married to Marie Antoinette, daughter of MARIA THERESA of Austria. He succeeded to a country impoverished by war and torn by class hatred. It would have needed a clever king and a strong one to cope; Louis, though well-intentioned, was neither. His natural shyness was not helped by a physical problem that left him unable to make love to his pretty young wife. Marie Antoinette, frustrated, turned her attention to court intrigue and politics. By the time a small operation had cured the king's disability, her interference in public affairs had become an established thing.

The only solution to the country's problems appeared to be to make the nobility pay taxes, from which they were exempt. France's affairs grew worse during the 1770s because it intervened on the side of the United States in its war of independence against England. Finally, matters came to a head: the nobles argued that drastic reforms could not be carried through unless the States General, the national parliament, were convened—and this assembly had not met since 1614. On the advice of his ministers, Louis convened the assembly in 1789.

If Louis had been strong enough to ally himself with the re-
formers in the States General against the nobility, all might have
been well, but he allowed himself to be influenced by the nobility
and by his wife. The States General consisted of three Estates:
the clergy, the nobles and the Third Estate—the representatives
of the middle classes. The Third Estate sought power equal to the
other two estates combined. Louis tried to oppose them. But the
Third Estate merely took the powers it was denied and the French
Revolution began.

Violence soon followed, beginning with the storming of the
Bastille, a fortress-prison, and continuing with the burning and
looting of the nobles' houses. A mob marched to Versailles and
dragged the king and his family back to Paris, under its control.
After eighteen months Louis tried to escape from France, as
many of the nobility had already done, but he was caught and
brought back to Paris. Louis and Marie Antoinette then embarked
on a policy of scheming to get aid from foreign countries. War
with Austria, the queen's mother-country, led to fresh violence
and Louis and his family were placed under arrest. Louis was
declared deposed and brought to trial for treason against the state.
A National Convention, elected by the people, heard the case and
condemned him to death. He was guillotined in January 1793.
Marie Antoinette was executed eight months later. Their young
son, whom royalists regarded as King Louis XVII after his
father's death, died in prison from disease and neglect at the age
of 10.

LOUIS PHILIPPE (1773–1850) was the last king of France. He
was a member of the French royal family of Bourbon but was not
in the direct line of descent. His great-great-great-grandfather
was Philippe, duc d'Orléans, younger son of LOUIS XIII. His
father, Philippe, duc d'Orléans, sympathised with the French
Revolution when it began, adopting the name of *Philippe
Égalité* (Equality—one of the watchwords of the Revolution).
Louis Philippe fought for a while in the French army, then, dis-

agreeing with the execution of Louis XVI—for which his father voted—went into exile. He spent some years in Switzerland, the United States and England. He finally returned to France when the monarchy was restored in 1815.

In 1830 Charles X, younger brother of LOUIS XVI, issued a series of *ordinances* (orders) muzzling the Press and changing the system of voting. This was the climax of a long struggle between the monarchy and the middle classes: a new revolution broke out and the rebels turned to Louis Philippe. On 9 August he was proclaimed king of the French. Charles X had fled.

Although Louis Philippe had been put on the throne by the people, not all of them supported him: there was an undercurrent of unrest. Many people favoured a return to a republican government; others supported the family of NAPOLEON I, now represented by his nephew Louis Napoleon (see NAPOLEON III). There was a series of republican and socialist uprisings, put down with difficulty. In 1836 Louis Napoleon tried to lead a rebellion; it failed and he had to flee the country. In his efforts to maintain his position, Louis Philippe adopted repressive measures and opposed reforms of the electoral system. Both these courses alienated his own supporters. Many Frenchmen were anxious for war with the German states, which Louis Philippe also opposed.

In 1848, a year in which revolutions broke out in many parts of Europe, a mob gathered to protest against the banning of a political banquet. This movement quickly became yet another insurrection. Louis Philippe abdicated in favour of his young grandson, also named Louis Philippe, but the people would have nothing to do with the boy, and a new republic was proclaimed. Louis Philippe fled to England, where he spent his last years.

MALCOLM III (*c.* 1031–1093) was the son of Duncan I of Scotland, who was killed by one of his subjects, Macbeth, in battle in 1040. Duncan was a weak king. Macbeth, who then took the throne, was a strong one; his claim to the throne was probably as strong as that of Duncan. While he ruled Malcolm was gathering strength, and enlisting the support of Earl Siward of Northumbria. In 1057 he defeated Macbeth in battle and killed him. A few months later, in 1058, he made himself king of the Scots. He was nicknamed *Canmore*—'big-head'.

Malcolm spent a large part of his youth at the court of Edward the Confessor of England and had many English friends. This did not stop him trying to take advantage of the chaos in England caused by the Norman invasion of 1066 and trying to seize parts of northern England. He did not succeed, but he gave shelter to two Saxon refugees, Edgar the Aethling and his sister Margaret, grandchildren of Edward's elder brother Edmund Ironside. In 1070 Malcolm married Margaret, a deeply religious woman who exerted a good influence on her husband and on the Scottish court. She was canonised as a saint in 1250.

Malcolm's habit of raiding south into England led WILLIAM THE CONQUEROR to exact homage from him in 1072. Malcolm also paid homage to the Conqueror's son, William Rufus, in 1093, but the 2 men mistrusted each other. Later in the year Malcolm was killed while invading England yet again. He was succeeded in turn by 3 of his sons, Edgar, Alexander I, and David I.

MARIA THERESA (1717–1780), Archduchess of Austria, was the centre of a storm that raged in Europe for 40 years of her life. She was the daughter and heir of the Holy Roman Emperor Charles VI, the last surviving male of the once mighty Habsburg family. In the 18th century the idea of a woman as ruler was not acceptable to many of the kings and princes of Europe. Foreseeing trouble, Charles issued in 1724 a decree called the *Pragmatic Sanction*, declaring Maria Theresa heir to all his lands, and persuading most of the rulers of central Europe to agree to it. In 1736 Maria Theresa married Francis, Duke of Lorraine, a minor European prince who had been brought up at Charles VI's court.

When Charles died in 1740 a number of European princes immediately claimed his lands, or part of them. They included Philip V of Spain, Frederick II of Prussia, and Augustus III of Saxony, all of whom had agreed to the Pragmatic Sanction, plus the Elector Charles Albert of Bavaria, who had not. France, Poland, Sardinia and Saxony all allied themselves with Prussia, in the War of the Austrian Succession. But with the support of Hungary—of which she was queen—Britain and the Netherlands, Maria Theresa managed to defend herself. When the war ended in 1748 Maria Theresa had to yield the province of Silesia to Prussia; but she gained the election of her husband as Holy Roman Emperor.

Maria Theresa was determined to win back Silesia, making secret treaties with France and Russia, hoping to overpower Prussia. But Frederick decided to attack first while the new, shaky alliance was unprepared and the Seven Years' War broke out in 1756. When it ended in 1763 Prussia still held Silesia.

In 1765 Francis died, and Maria Theresa's son Joseph II was elected as emperor and co-ruler of Austria with her. The empress introduced a number of reforms in education and in the life and treatment of the poorest classes, the serfs. Another succession war broke out in 1778 when the last Elector of Bavaria died without a direct heir. Joseph tried to gain Bavaria for Austria but was frustrated by Frederick of Prussia, though no battles were fought.

Among Maria Theresa's 16 children was the Archduchess Marie Antoinette, who married LOUIS XVI of France.

MARY, QUEEN OF SCOTS (1542–1587), was one of the most unfortunate sovereigns who ever lived. Badly trained and badly advised, she was the focus of plots that proved her undoing. Mary was the only legitimate child of King James V of Scotland, a member of the unlucky Stuart family. James came to the throne at the age of 17 months and died at 30 just a week after Mary was born. Her mother, a French princess, had her brought up in France from the age of 6. This upbringing was the beginning of her misfortunes: she was trained to be a devout Roman Catholic at a time when her own country was becoming fiercely Protestant.

At the age of 16 Mary married the French dauphin (crown prince), who became king as Francis II a year later. He was a sickly young man and died 18 months later. There was no place for Mary at the court of her 10-year-old brother-in-law, the new king, Charles IX. She decided to return to Scotland.

Mary arrived in Scotland at the age of 19, a pretty, sophisticated, clever girl, used to the wit and gaiety of the French court. She found the Scots a dour people, all the more so for the Calvinistic religion so many of them had adopted, and the land a grey one after France. At first, with the aid of her illegitimate half-brother, the Earl of Moray, she contrived to rule sensibly. But her contempt of the Scots soon affected the conduct of her affairs.

A more important influence on Mary was the fact that she was the heir apparent to ELIZABETH I of England. In her own eyes indeed she was England's rightful queen, because Roman Catholics did not recognise HENRY VIII's marriage to Anne Boleyn, Elizabeth's mother. This constituted a threat to Elizabeth's position; as a result the English kept a very watchful eye on Mary's activities. It was with a view to strengthening her claim to the English throne that Mary decided in 1565 to marry her cousin Henry Stuart, Lord Darnley, who could also stake a claim to the English throne. Darnley was also a Roman Catholic. The marriage upset the Protestant nobility of Scotland, including Moray, who tried to lead a revolt; but Mary's supporters drove Moray and his friends over the border into England.

Darnley was a tall, handsome, man but weak and conceited. Mary soon tired of him. She made a friend of her Italian secretary, David Rizzio, and this aroused Darnley, who then readily agreed to support a conspiracy to get rid of Rizzio. A group of Scottish lords did this in the most barbarous way, stabbing Rizzio to death in front of Mary in the Palace of Holyroodhouse, Edinburgh. The bloodstains can still be seen on the floor of the room where the murder was done. Mary made her escape, aided by Darnley, and sought the help of a loyal Scottish soldier, James Hepburn, Earl of Bothwell. Escorted by Bothwell and an army, she returned to Edinburgh to confront Rizzio's murderers. To her horror they showed her proof that Darnley was a fellow conspirator. Mary tried to reconcile herself to Darnley but found the task distasteful. A few weeks later she gave birth to a son, later JAMES I AND VI.

In 1567 Mary and Darnley, who was ill, arranged to spend a few nights at Kirk o'Field, a half-ruined house on the outskirts of Edinburgh. On 9 February Mary left the house to attend a party and during the night an explosion blew the house to pieces. Darnley was found dead—strangled. The Scots suspected Bothwell of having contrived the murder, so when Mary married Bothwell a few weeks later their indignation knew no bounds. A rebel army defeated her loyal forces at the battle of Carberry Hill, the nobles offering Mary the choice of giving up the throne or being accused of murder. Mary surrendered the throne in favour of her baby son and was imprisoned.

The following year she escaped and again raised an army to fight for her. Another defeat followed, and Mary fled over the border to England to ask sanctuary from Elizabeth. She had escaped from one prison to another as Elizabeth did not feel safe with Mary, a rival claimant to the throne, at large. So at the age of 25 Mary's freedom came to an end; for 20 years she was kept in captivity, the focus of Roman Catholic plots. Twice Elizabeth had proof of Mary's involvement in plots against her life and twice she spared her against the advice of the English parliament and ministers. Finally, in 1586, another plot was uncovered. This time Mary was brought to trial for treason and found guilty. Elizabeth's ministers persuaded her to sign the death warrant, urging that Mary was a danger to the State. Mary died as she had lived, with courage and grace.

MAXIMILIAN I (1459–1519), Holy Roman Emperor, built up the fortunes of the Habsburg family and also began the process of uniting Germany that was finally completed in the reign of the Prussian king, WILLIAM I. Maximilian was the son of the Emperor Frederick III. In 1477 he married Mary, daughter of Charles the Bold, Duke of Burgundy, although Charles was killed in battle in the same year. Maximilian tried to defend his wife's inheritance in Burgundy and the Netherlands against attack by the French, but lost Burgundy. In 1486 he was chosen king of the Romans, which meant he was heir presumptive to the empire. Four years later he returned to Germany to recapture Vienna from the Hungarians, whose king, Matthias I Corvinus, had just died. Two years later he routed the Turks, and won victories against the French. In 1493, on the death of his father, he became emperor.

Maximilian's reign was full of wars and battles, in which he had mixed success. He took for his second wife the daughter of the Duke of Milan, but eventually had to concede Milan to the French. In 1499 the Swiss won their independence from him.

It was in the field of diplomacy that Maximilian scored his greatest victories, and in making advantageous marriages for his family. In 1496 his son Philip married the Infanta Joan of Spain; their son became the Emperor CHARLES V, and the marriage brought the great Spanish possessions under Habsburg rule. His grandson Ferdinand was married to the daughter of the Hungarian king, and this marriage brought Hungary and Bohemia into the family.

Maximilian has been called 'the last of the knights', from his notions of chivalry and adventure. He was something of a dreamer and a scholar, and encouraged the development of the arts in the empire. He wrote his own autobiography, glorifying and romanticising his career, besides works on hunting and gardening. He even had a notion of ending the long struggle between popes and emperors by becoming pope himself, though this may not have been a serious idea. He was the first emperor to take the title without being crowned at Rome, and from this time the Holy Roman Empire lost all connections with Rome or holiness and became a purely German institution.

MONTEZUMA II (1466–1520) was the last Aztec Emperor of Mexico. As a prince he was trained both for the priesthood and as a warrior. He was elected to succeed his uncle in 1502. His prowess as a soldier was so great that he was a member of an order, the Quachictin, to which only great warriors were admitted, and only one other emperor belonged. He was present at 9 battles. By a mixture of warfare and diplomacy he enlarged his empire. He lived in an atmosphere of pomp and luxury, and everything was going well for him when the Spaniards under the *conquistador* Hernán Cortés landed.

The Aztec religion had a prophecy that its great god Quetzalcoatl, bearded and white of skin, was due to return. Cortés appeared to be that god, and Montezuma, the proud and courageous, welcomed Cortés humbly and graciously. He became a prisoner of the Spaniards. Many of his people, however, were not so awed, and began a rebellion against their new conquerors. Montezuma harangued the mob from the battlements of his palace, but the crowd shouted 'The white men have made you a coward!' and launched a shower of stones. One of them struck Montezuma on the head. He died soon afterwards, partly from his wound and partly from a broken heart.

MUTSUHITO (1852–1912) was an emperor of Japan who helped his country to develop into a modern state. He is also known by his adopted reign title as *Meiji*. Mutsuhito succeeded his father, Komei, in 1867, when he was only 15 years old. At that time Japan was under the control of the *shoguns*, the feudal lords who had ruled the country since the AD 700s. The shoguns opposed allowing foreigners into the country to trade. Soon after Mutsuhito came to the throne the last shogun, Keiki, was persuaded to resign. With the aid of loyal advisers, the young emperor assumed direct control as ruler, transferring the country's capital from Kyoto to Edo, which he renamed Tokyo, 'Eastern capital'. In 1871 he abolished feudalism.

Under Mutsuhito's dynamic leadership the country began to adopt western ideas of government and a rapid programme of industrialisation was started. During the 1870s Japan adopted the Gregorian calendar, opened its first railway, remodelled its navy with advice from British officers and adopted a policy of religious toleration. A central bank was founded in 1882, and a Diet (parliament) in 1889. The social revolution was so great that at one time it seemed traditional Japanese customs would all fall into abeyance. Within a few years Japan had been transformed from a medieval country, cut off from the rest of the world, into a wealthy leading power—a position it has held ever since. There is some doubt as to whether the early part of this revolution was the result of Mutsuhito's own ideas, but by the end of the reign he and his advisers were certainly working very closely together. During the reign the Japanese fought and won wars against China (1895) and Russia (1905).

NAPOLEON I (1769–1821) was a Corsican soldier who made himself emperor of the French and master of most of Europe by the time he was 38. Eight years later he went into a lonely exile, his meteoric career finished.

Napoleon Buonaparte was born at Ajaccio, the capital of Corsica, the second of 5 brothers and 3 sisters; 5 other children died in infancy. Like most Corsicans, he was of Italian descent. Napoleon's father, a lawyer and a member of the nobility, sent him to school and then to a military academy in France. He studied hard, but spent long periods of leave in Corsica, planning how to liberate it from French rule. When the French Revolution broke out Napoleon welcomed it as offering Corsica its freedom and himself a chance of promotion. The Corsicans won, not independence, but incorporation with France with full privileges of citizenship, which satisfied them. Napoleon was dismissed from the army for making violent speeches, but soon talked his way back in.

As a captain of artillery, Napoleon won acclaim at the siege of Toulon by British and Spanish fleets. He was promoted to brigadier-general, but soon afterwards was arrested as a supporter of Maximilien Robespierre, leader of the dreaded Reign of Terror in which thousands of people perished on the guillotine. However, nothing could be proved and Napoleon was freed. In October,

1795, he used artillery to dispel a mob that was attacking the National Convention, a kind of parliament. He referred to it as a 'whiff of grapeshot'. It brought him swift promotion to be commander-in-chief of the French armies in Italy, and a general.

Before he left for Italy Napoleon married Josephine de Beauharnais, the beautiful widow of a nobleman who had been guillotined. Each thought the other was wealthy and did not discover the truth until they were married. However, Josephine brought Napoleon influential friends and also helped him to live down his Corsican background, which was a handicap to his career. He also adopted a French form of his surname, *Bonaparte*.

Before he left Paris Napoleon had been working on plans to drive the Austrians, with whom France was at war, out of Italy. He proceeded to put them into brilliant effect, winning a series of victories. Ignoring the government in Paris, he proceeded to make peace with the Austrians, created 2 new republics in Italy under French rule and returned to Paris in triumph. In the campaign he captured enough booty to pay his soldiers and make himself a wealthy man.

In Paris a 5 man government called the Directory ruled France; its members trusted Napoleon and readily agreed with a plan he put forward for invading Egypt, with a view to striking at British interests in India. Within a few weeks Napoleon had won the battle of the Pyramids (1798) and made himself master of Egypt. Then a British fleet under Horatio Nelson attacked and destroyed the French fleet that had taken Napoleon's armies to Egypt, cutting him off. Napoleon tried to invade Palestine, with little success. After this, hearing that the government in Paris was in difficulties, he abandoned his army and sailed for home, receiving a hero's welcome. With his friends, he dominated the Assembly (parliament) and had the constitution changed to provide for a government by 3 consuls, himself and 2 older men. The final *coup d'état* which placed him in power took place on 9 November 1799. It is known as the *coup d'état de Brumaire*, because it happened in the month of Brumaire in the short-lived Revolutionary Calendar.

The new First Consul soon proved that he was as good an administrator as he was a general. He reorganised the government, set up a new code of laws, the *Code Napoléon*, which is still the basis of French law, and founded the *Légion d'Honneur* to reward his brave soldiers.

Several nations were still ranged against France, and Napoleon determined to knock them out one by one. In 1800 he marched into northern Italy and defeated the Austrians again at the battle of Marengo. Soon afterwards, Britain made peace and France had no war for the first time for 10 years. In 1802, to gain some much-needed funds, Napoleon sold the French colonies in North America, the Louisiana Territory, to the United States, knowing he could not defend them anyway.

In 1802 Napoleon was voted First Consul for life. Two years later the Senate, the upper house of the French parliament, voted to offer him the title of emperor, having been carefully primed to do so: the republic was ended. At his lavish coronation Napoleon had the pope to perform the ceremony, but placed the crown on his own head to show it was his by right of conquest.

Austria, Britain, Russia and Sweden began a new campaign against France in 1805, alarmed by Napoleon's obvious ambition. Napoleon crushed the Austrian and Russian armies at the battles of Ulm and Austerlitz, and though Nelson's defeat of the French fleet at Trafalgar made Britain safe, Napoleon was free to do as he pleased in Europe. He abolished the Holy Roman Empire, made his brothers kings of Spain, Holland and Westphalia, annexed large parts of Germany to France and generally redrew the map of Europe as he pleased. Prussia resisted, and was crushed at the battles of Jena and Auerstädt. He also issued the Berlin Decrees, forbidding trade with Britain.

In 1810, needing an heir which Josephine was unable to give him, Napoleon divorced her and married the Archduchess Marie Louise of Austria, by whom he had a son. Two years later, he decided to launch a campaign against Russia, which was showing signs of independence. It was his greatest mistake: the Russian armies were no match for him, but the Russian winter was. He captured Moscow, which had been abandoned and set on fire, and then found himself snowbound with no supplies. In the retreat from Moscow he lost almost all his army of 600,000 men. Meanwhile in Spain a combined British and Spanish force kept many valuable troops tied down—a 'running sore in France's side', as it has been called. France's enemies made a new effort to bring Napoleon down. He raised a fresh army and fought them off, but in 1813 he was defeated at the battle of the Nations, at Leipzig. His commanders insisted that he should abdicate so that they could make peace. In April, 1814, he gave up the throne, and was exiled—still with the title of emperor—to the small Mediterranean island of Elba.

In February 1815 reports reached him of discontent with the new ruler of France, Louis XVIII; he decided to return. He was welcomed with cheers, the king fleeing. His old soldiers flocked to him, and he was declared emperor again. As a reaction the British, Dutch, Belgians and Germans assembled an army, but Napoleon at once marched to crush it before it grew too strong. He defeated the Prussians at the battle of Ligny, and seemed poised for another series of victories. However, 2 days later when he attacked the British and their allies at Waterloo, in Belgium, he was utterly routed after a day-long slaughter. This time he was exiled to the lonely Atlantic island of St Helena, where he died 6 years later.

NAPOLEON III (1808–1873) became the second emperor of the French. He was the son of NAPOLEON I's younger brother Louis Bonaparte, King of Holland. He was named *Charles Louis Napoleon*, and was known as *Louis Napoleon* for many years. With all the other members of the Bonaparte family, Louis Napoleon was exiled from France by the returning king, Louis XVIII, and spent his youth in various European countries. His uncle was his great hero, and he constantly plotted to retrieve the family fortunes. His father and his uncles had no wish to claim the throne of France, and in 1832 Napoleon I's only son, Napoleon II, Duke of Reichstadt, died, leaving Louis Napoleon as the sole pretender.

In 1836 Louis Napoleon tried to start a rebellion at Strasbourg. It failed, and the French deported him to the United States. He returned to Europe, settling in England, where he poured forth a stream of propaganda designed to prepare the way to the throne. In 1840 he landed at Boulogne and tried to start another rebellion. This time the king, LOUIS PHILIPPE, had him brought to trial. Sentenced to life imprisonment, he spent 5 years in jail before escaping in disguise and making his way back to England.

The Revolution of 1848 which overthrew Louis Philippe gave Louis Napoleon his opportunity. He returned to France, was at once elected to the Assembly, and decided to stand for election to the presidency of the new republic; he was elected by a large majority. The new president was given powers similar to those of the president of the United States. He used them to appoint his friends and supporters to important posts. The president was to serve for 4 years. In 1851 Louis Napoleon out-manoeuvred the new parliament by demanding that it should give the vote to 3 million peasants who did not have it. When parliament refused Louis Napoleon dissolved it, held a plebiscite and persuaded the people of France to vote him a 10-year term of office with unlimited powers. He appointed a council of state to make laws, and a senate to reject any that were unconstitutional. The senate, supported by yet another plebiscite, declared Napoleon to be emperor.

Napoleon III's foreign policy was designed to make France great again, if possible by peaceful means. In 1853 he led his country into an alliance with the old enemy, Britain, to support Turkey against Russia in the Crimean War. He also gave aid to Italian patriots who were fighting against Austrian rule, but being a devout Roman Catholic supported the pope against them when they wanted to seize Rome. The only real advantage he gained was the transfer of the provinces of Nice and Savoy from Italy to

France. An attempt to put the Austrian Prince Maximilian on the throne of Mexico in 1864 ended in disaster.

Napoleon wanted to regain some of the territories France had lost after the defeat of Napoleon I. This led to a clash of interests with Prussia, which had become the most powerful German state. In 1870 Prussia supported the nomination of a German prince to be king of Spain; Napoleon demanded that the prince withdraw his claim. This was agreed, but the French insisted on guarantees that Prussia would never support a renewal of the claim. The Prussian king, WILLIAM I, refused, and his chief minister, Prince Otto von Bismarck, published the refusal reworded in brusque terms. France and Napoleon took this as an insult and at once declared war.

Unfortunately for Napoleon, the Prussian army was organised and well led, while the French army was neither. Napoleon himself, though a sick man, insisted on leading his forces. On 2 September 1870, just 43 days after France had declared war, the emperor and a large French force were surrounded at Sedan and had to surrender. Dissatisfaction with Napoleon's rule had been growing in France, and this news brought about his downfall. Within 2 days the Third Republic was proclaimed, Napoleon, released by the Germans, retiring once more to England, where he died 3 years later. His only son, the Prince Imperial Napoleon Eugène Louis, joined a British expedition to Zululand in 1879 to gain military experience, but was killed in an ambush by the Zulus.

NEBUCHADREZZAR II (died 562 BC) was the most powerful king of Babylon. He was the son of Nabopolassar, who founded the Chaldean dynasty in Babylonia and crushed the kingdom of Assyria. His name is sometimes spelled *Nebuchadnezzar*. As crown prince he led Babylonia's armies in the west, defeating the Egyptians and winning from them Palestine and Syria. He hurried back to Babylon in 605 BC when his father died, in order to claim the throne.

In 598 BC the Jewish kingdom of Judah rebelled against its

new conquerors. Nebuchadrezzar marched an army into Judah, captured Jerusalem and took as prisoners the King of Judah, Jehoiachin, together with his family and many other Jews. Clay tablets found in the ruins of Babylon record the regular issue of rations to the prisoners. In Jehoiachin's place Nebuchadrezzar set up his young uncle, Mattaniah, as a puppet-king, renaming him Zedekiah. In 587 BC Zedekiah also rebelled. Nebuchadrezzar returned and again attacked Jerusalem. This time the Jews resisted for 2 years. When the city finally fell, Nebuchadrezzar destroyed the temple and many other buildings and took a very large number of Jews back to Babylon as captives.

The Babylonians also besieged the Phoenician city of Tyre, whose ruins lie in modern Lebanon. This siege lasted 13 years. When Tyre finally fell in 572 BC Nebuchadrezzar ruled over an empire that stretched from the Persian Gulf to the Mediterranean Sea. Under his rule Babylon became a centre of trade, art and learning. He built a magnificent palace whose roof gardens were included by the Greeks in the Seven Wonders of the World. These gardens were watered by pumps worked by relays of slaves. Oil from the petroleum-rich soil was used to light the city at night. In his last years of life Nebuchadrezzar suffered from fits of madness, in which he imagined he was an animal and ate grass.

NERO (AD 37–68) was one of the most debauched emperors of Rome. He was the son of Gnaeus Domitius Ahenobarbus, a Roman noble, and Agrippina, niece of the emperor Claudius. His father died when he was 3 and 9 years later Agrippina married Claudius. She persuaded Claudius to make Nero, rather than his own son, his heir, and to marry Nero to his daughter Octavia. In 54 Claudius died of poison, administered, it is said, by Agrippina, and Nero became emperor at the age of 17.

The early years of Nero's reign were marked by good government, because he acted on the advice of his tutor, Lucius Annaeus Seneca, and Sextus Afranius Burrus, a prefect. While they ran the empire for him, Nero was free to indulge in every kind of folly and vice. He loved singing, believed he had a fine voice and used to take part in concerts and theatrical performances. He took part in singing contests and chariot races, in which he was always the winner. At night he would go on the rampage in the streets, attacking passers-by and looting shops; his sex-life was a public scandal.

In 58 he fell in love with Poppaea, wife of a dissolute Roman nobleman. Agrippina protested at the affair, so Nero had her put to death. He then divorced Octavia (who was murdered soon after), sent Otho to govern Lusitania (Portugal) and married Poppaea. Three years later he kicked her dead because she dared to complain when he came home late from the races.

About this period of his life Nero's mind became unbalanced. His vices grew more unusual and unpleasant; he suspected plots at every turn and had many noblemen put to death for allegedly scheming against him. When Rome caught fire in 64, a disastrous blaze that destroyed half the city, he watched the flames entranced, playing the lyre and chanting a long Greek poem. Small wonder that many Romans believed the false rumour that Nero had started the fire himself. Finally hatred for Nero grew so great that the Roman armies revolted. Nero fled from Rome and took refuge in a friend's villa. There he heard he would be flogged to death if caught. Ordering his servants to prepare his grave, he muttered 'Dead! And so great an artist!' and after several hesitations cut his throat.

NICHOLAS II (1868–1918) was the last tsar of Russia. He was the son of Alexander III. As tsarevich (heir to the throne) Nicholas gave the impression of being weak, but this was belied by the resolve with which he defied his father's wishes in order to marry the girl of his choice. She was Princess Alice of Hessen-Darmstadt, who adopted the name of Alexandra on her marriage. She had been brought up in England by her grandmother, Queen VICTORIA, and her natural shyness concealed great determination. Nicholas succeeded his father in 1894, continuing the tradition of autocratic rule, and concealing his intention to have his own way behind his natural charm and good manners. However, he could be swayed by his advisers, their counsel leading him into war against Japan in 1904, which brought a humiliating defeat to Russia. The country, which had seemed quiet when he came to the throne, exploded into revolution in 1905, with riots and widespread strikes. The tsar was glad to promise political reforms, including freedom of speech and more democratic rule, to secure peace. In accordance with this pledge he set up a parliamentary body, the Duma, but eventually it had much less power than expected. The result of the reforms was a good deal more real freedom for the people, and much less revolutionary activity.

In 1914 Russia was drawn into war against Austria and Germany, ostensibly in defence of Serbia. At first the people were whole-heartedly behind their tsar, but unpreparedness for war brought a series of shattering defeats. Corruption among Nicholas's ministers aggravated an already grave situation and revolutionary activities flared up once more. People were suspicious of Alexandra because she was German by birth. They also distrusted her reliance on religious cranks and imposters, such as the monk Grigori Rasputin. Rasputin's main hold over her was his ability to control bleeding in the Tsarevich Alexis, who had inherited the family disease of haemophilia. Eventually a group of aristocrats assassinated Rasputin. In the early part of 1917 a series of riots broke out because of food shortages. Attempts by the army to suppress them failed, and Nicholas's whole system of government suddenly collapsed. He was forced to abdicate, and he and his family were kept under arrest. In July 1918 the new Communist rulers of Russia had the whole family put to death.

OTTO I, THE GREAT (912–973), was the real creator of the Holy Roman Empire, though it did not then have that name. He succeeded his father, HENRY I, the Fowler, as German king in 936. He held his coronation at Aachen, CHARLEMAGNE's capital, and 4 dukes attended him at the ceremony. Their attendance did

not make them obedient subjects, however, and Otto fought a
3-year campaign to assert his royal authority over them. He then
quelled 2 rebellions in which his younger brother, Henry, was a
ringleader. In a later revolt his own son, Liudolf, took part. All
these internal quarrels Otto dealt with efficiently, leaving himself
free for further expansion.

In 955 Otto faced the Magyars of Hungary, who had been
threatening Germany for many years, and defeated them at the
battle of Lechfeld. This was a decisive battle: the Magyars never
again menaced German territory. Otto had already led a successful
expedition into Italy and claimed the Italian crown. The pope,
Agapetus II, refused to crown him as emperor; but in 960
Agapetus's successor, John XII, appealed to Otto for help against
his own rebellious subjects. This time Otto claimed the imperial
crown as his reward. He also insisted that he must be consulted
in the election of any future pope. When John XII began negotiating with Otto's enemies, the emperor deposed him and made
Leo VIII pope instead. He also nominated Leo's successor, John
XIII, 2 years later.

By his actions Otto not only revived the empire which Charlemagne had founded, but made it a strong and comparatively
united one. He also began a cultural revival, encouraging literature. While he exerted his authority over the Church he also
strengthened its position.

PETER I, THE GREAT (1672–1725), modernised Russia and
made it one of the great powers of the world. Peter was the son of
Tsar Alexis (reigned 1645–76) by his second marriage. When
Alexis died his eldest son, Theodore III, succeeded him—a
chronic invalid who died at the age of 20. Theodore's full brother,
Ivan V, followed him, but since he was feeble-minded Peter was
made joint tsar at the age of 10; Ivan's sister, Sophia, made herself
regent. Peter spent much of his boyhood away from the court,
learning to sail and build boats besides many other handicrafts.

In 1689 Peter staged a *coup d'état*, deposed his half-sister and assumed power. He allowed Ivan V to live quietly until he died in 1696. As ruling tsar, Peter was able to indulge his passion for war games, which he played with regiments of soldiers. Out of these games came a campaign against the Turks at Azov, on the Black Sea, which after an initial reverse gave Russia a Black Sea port for the first time.

In 1697–98 Peter made a tour of western Europe, travelling part of the time incognito, though with a large suite. He took a lively interest in all things technical, such as saw-mills, shipyards and military defences. He even worked for a week as a carpenter in a Dutch port. He returned to Russia to suppress a revolt of the royal guards, which he did with the utmost severity, 2,000 men being executed. His half-sister Sophia, who was behind the revolt, was forced to become a nun. He meted the same punishment to his own wife, also involved in the revolt.

For the next 20 years Peter was engaged in the Great Northern War against Sweden, in which his opponent was CHARLES XII. He defeated Charles at the battle of Poltava in 1709 and secured an outlet to the Gulf of Finland, on the Baltic Sea. In this region he had already founded a new city, St Petersburg (Leningrad), which he made his capital. Peter also fought wars against Turkey and Persia.

Peter's reforms were far-reaching: he compelled his people to wear a more western style of dress, reorganised the civil service, created a navy, revitalised the army, developed industries such as textile manufacture and mining, encouraged trade and built roads and canals. He founded a number of schools and reformed the Russian alphabet. A lover of all things western, he made the court and the aristocracy follow western ways, which helped to estrange them from the peasants who were left following traditional Russian ways. He enforced the rule of law by barbarous punishments. When his son and heir, Alexis, turned against him, Peter accused him of treason and had him jailed and flogged. Alexis died from the flogging before he could face trial.

Peter was a giant of a man, 6 feet 6 inches (2m) tall, possessed of a colossal and destructive energy. He could drink like a fish and still be sober enough to work. He used the same vigour in working with his hands, horseplay with his friends or drafting state papers. He had many mistresses, finally marrying one of them, a Lithuanian servant girl named Martha Skavronskaya, who took the name of Catherine. Catherine was a jolly, bawdy girl, who could soothe Peter when he flew into a rage. After his death she succeeded him to rule as empress in her own right. She survived him by only 2 years.

PHILIP II, AUGUSTUS (1165–1223), King of France, made the French monarchy powerful for the first time, and won for the crown the enormous areas of France that were under the control of the English kings. He was the son of Louis VII, and in 1179 was crowned as joint king with his father, who was a dying man. Louis died a year later.

Philip inherited a strange and dangerous situation: although he was king of France, a number of more or less powerful barons held various parts of the country as vassals of the king. This might not have been so bad; but one vassal held more than half of France—and he was also HENRY II, King of England. Henry had inherited England through his mother; from his father he inherited Normandy and Anjou; and his wife, Eleanor, brought him the duchy of Aquitaine. Philip made a 6-year treaty with Henry, which left him free to exert his authority over some of his other vassals. Having done that, he then encouraged Henry's rebellious sons to rise against their father.

When Henry died in 1189, Philip made friends with his son RICHARD I, and the 2 kings went off to Palestine together on the Third Crusade, where they quarrelled. When Richard was taken prisoner by the ruler of Austria, Duke Leopold, Philip did everything he could to make sure the English king stayed a captive. In 1194 Richard was ransomed, and at once set about fighting to guard his French possessions. A successful 5 year campaign ended with the death of Richard, and Philip found his successor, John, a much less formidable foe. In a series of campaigns he captured Normandy, Maine, Touraine and Anjou. In 1214 Philip delivered his final stroke—the battle of Bouvines—finally crushing John's hopes of retaining any of his territory except a small part of Aquitaine. A further important result of the wars was that the captured lands came directly under the French king, thus making him a much more powerful person than any of his barons.

Philip, who was known as *Augustus* because of his wisdom, was also known as a 'second founder' of Paris because of the great building works he carried out there. He built the Louvre as his royal palace and founded the University of Paris.

PHILIP II (1527–1598), the only son of the emperor CHARLES V, succeeded his father as king of Spain in 1556, the title of emperor going to his uncle, Ferdinand. Philip also inherited the Netherlands, much of northern Italy and Spain's vast overseas empire. He was a quiet, dour man, a fanatical Roman Catholic and bureaucrat who liked to govern with the aid of letters and memoranda. In the 1560s he built the Escorial, near Madrid, a combined palace, convent and church. Inside this enormous building Philip had a small private suite, where he spent his time in a cheerless, isolated room that served him as an office, and might almost have been a monk's cell.

Philip's first wife, Maria of Portugal, died giving birth to a son. His second wife was Mary I of England, which made him joint ruler of that country until Mary died in 1558. He later married a French princess, Elizabeth of Valois, and finally Anna of Austria.

For Philip, his religion mattered more than anything else, and this coloured his home and foreign policy. He encouraged the Inquisition to ferret out heretics and unbelievers. He tried to impose Roman Catholicism on the Netherlands, which drove the Dutch to rebel against Spain. He was resolutely opposed to the Protestant ruler of England, Mary's half-sister ELIZABETH I, and supported plots to put MARY, QUEEN OF SCOTS, on the English throne. After Elizabeth had Mary executed Philip determined to invade England. He despatched an army, carried by a fleet known as the Invincible Armada. The Armada was not, however, invincible, and the English fleet, aided by bad weather, destroyed it. Philip tried to intervene in France to prevent that country coming under Protestant rule, but was outmanoeuvred by the Protestant leader, Henry of Navarre, who became a Roman Catholic when he succeeded to the throne as HENRY IV.

Philip's greatest triumph was the decisive defeat of the Turks by a combined Spanish and Italian fleet at the battle of Lepanto in 1571. It ended the Muslim threat to Christian Europe. The battle was won by Philip's illegitimate half-brother, Don John of Austria.

RAMESES II (died 1237 BC) was one of Egypt's greatest pharaohs (kings) and certainly one of its greatest builders. He succeeded his father, Seti I, in 1304 BC, and soon after began a campaign against the Hittites, a people who ruled in Asia Minor (modern Turkey) and were gradually expanding south into Syria. A great battle was fought at Kadesh, which both sides claimed as a victory. After several years of desultory fighting, Rameses made a treaty with the Hittites and married a Hittite princess.

Rameses had an insatiable appetite for building: a great many temples were constructed during his reign, the most remarkable being the rock temple of Abu Simbel, whose original site is now under the waters of Lake Nasser. Gigantic statues of the pharaoh are still standing all over Egypt. Rameses was not above capitalising on other men's work and he had his cipher carved on many older buildings, to the puzzlement of present-day archaeologists. A great deal of forced labour was needed to carry out the royal building programme; among those being made to work were the Israelites, who had fled into Egypt at a time of famine some hundreds of years earlier. The Israelites were set to build 2 store cities, named in the Bible as Raamses and Pithom. The ruins of Pithom have been found about 60 miles (96km) from Cairo, and

G

those of Raamses 30 miles (48km) from Port Said. The Israelites under Moses fled from Egypt about 1290 BC.

RICHARD I (1157–1199), the third son of HENRY II, became king of England on his father's death in 1189. He was a mixture of a knight of chivalry and an irresponsible, disloyal and hasty-tempered rebel. He had unlimited physical strength and courage, which earned for him the nickname of *Coeur de Lion*—the Lion-Hearted. From the age of 11 he held the Duchy of Aquitaine, which had belonged to his mother. At 15 he joined his brothers Henry and Geoffrey in a rebellion against their father, which the king crushed. In 1189, when his elder brothers William and Henry were both dead and he was the heir to England, Richard joined the French king Philip II in a further rebellion, soon after which Henry died.

Richard confirmed in their offices all those men who had been loyal to Henry, and set off on the Third Crusade, with several European princes including Philip II. The Crusaders won many battles against the Muslims, thanks largely to Richard's personal courage and generalship; but they quarrelled among themselves. Philip went home, and soon after when Richard heard news of unrest in England he had to make peace with the Muslim leader, SALADIN, and follow suit. Shipwrecked in the Adriatic, he tried to travel overland through Austria, but its duke, Leopold, with whom Richard had quarrelled in Palestine, had him arrested and imprisoned. His whereabouts were discovered, according to legend, by his faithful minstrel Blondel, who sang the king's favourite ditty outside a succession of castles until at last he was rewarded by hearing Richard sing in answer from his prison. The English paid a huge ransom to free Richard, who returned in 1194 to find his younger brother John in revolt against him. Richard chased John out of the country, raised an army and went over to France to defend his French possessions against Philip II, now openly an enemy. There, 5 years later, he died of a wound received while besieging a castle.

Although Richard spent only a few months of his 10-year reign in England, the country was well-governed by wise officers of state in his absence; their rule was possibly better than Richard's would have been.

The year of Richard's accession, 1189, is an important one in English law. Precedents and ownership of property that are based on long-established usage are deemed to run from 'time whereof the memory of man runneth not to the contrary', and that time is 1189. English legal memory stops short there.

ROBERT I, THE BRUCE (1274–1329), was a tireless fighter for Scotland's independence. The Bruces were a Norman family, one of whom married Isabel, younger daughter of a Scottish prince, David, Earl of Huntingdon. In 1290 the 7-year-old Queen Margaret, known as the *Maid of Norway* because her mother was married to the Norwegian king, died and the Scottish throne became vacant. The nearest heirs were the descendants of David, Earl of Huntingdon. Edward I of England, asked to decide, chose John Balliol, grandson of David's elder daughter. Edward expected Balliol to be his vassal, and when Balliol eventually rebelled, dethroned him. English rule prevailed for several years, despite a gallant uprising led by William Wallace, an outlaw knight.

In 1306 Robert Bruce, now 32, decided to make a bid for the vacant throne. He began by meeting his chief rival, John 'the Red' Comyn, in a church at Dumfries. He emerged, saying cheerfully 'I doubt me I've killed the Red Comyn'. Six weeks later he had himself crowned as king at Scone, traditional site of Scottish coronations. The ageing Edward I led an intensive campaign to crush Bruce, who was disastrously defeated and driven to take refuge on a lonely island off Ireland. There, according to legend, he saw a spider working tirelessly to build a web, despite all obstacles, and was heartened to carry on the struggle. He returned to Scotland, and in a long series of battles gradually recaptured lands and castles from the English.

In 1314 Edward I's weak and incompetent son, Edward II, led a large army into Scotland to try to subdue Bruce. It numbered more than 25,000 men. Bruce, with only 10,000 troops, awaited the English in a strong position, easily defended and protected in front by a small stream, the Bannock burn. Badly led, the English fell into confusion, breaking and fleeing when Bruce's camp followers appeared on a distant hill waving banners and making sounds like a large army. The English did not recognise Bruce's authority as king until 1328, but from Bannockburn onwards he was master of Scotland. He spent the rest of his life putting the country's affairs in order once more.

RUDOLF I (1218–1291) was the first member of the Habsburg family to rule Austria. From the time he became German king in 1273, the Habsburgs played a leading part in European history until the establishment of the Austrian Republic in 1918. The Habsburgs took their name from the Habichtsburg—Hawk's Castle—built by the family in 1020 on the banks of the Aar in Switzerland.

The power of the German kings, most of whom also held the title of emperor of the Holy Roman Empire, declined during the early 1200s, the death of Conrad IV in 1254 marking the start of a period of disorder, called the *Great Interregnum* by historians. During this time the great families of Germany were jockeying for position. With no central government to keep control princes and powerful Churchmen fought each other for lands, bands of robber knights infested the highways and trade was hampered. The 7 princes known as Electors, who had the responsibility of choosing the German king, quarrelled among themselves and contrived to elect 2 foreigners, an English prince and a Spanish prince. Neither was able to reign. Finally the pope, Gregory X, alarmed by the anarchy, threatened to nominate a king himself. So the Electors hurriedly chose Rudolf, Count of Habsburg.

Rudolf restored some sort of order in Germany, ending the

many private wars that were raging, and enforcing the law. He defeated a rival claimant to the throne, Otakar II of Bohemia, and made alliances to safeguard his territories. He was unable to be crowned emperor at Rome, thanks to the intervention of the French. He made the Habsburg family both rich and powerful—so much so that when he died the Electors deliberately chose another prince, Adolf of Nassau, to succeed him. However, Rudolf's son Albert, whom he had made Duke of Austria, overthrew Adolf 6 years later and was elected as king.

SALADIN (1138–1193) was the first sultan of Egypt and Syria of the Ayyubid dynasty. The dynasty ruled until 1238. Saladin is the westernised form of *Salah al-Din Yusaf ibn-Ayyud*. He was the son of Ayyub, governor of Damascus, from whom the dynasty takes its name. Saladin began his career in the service of Nured-din, Sultan of Syria, a fanatical warrior dedicated to the cause of the *jihad* (holy war) against the Christians. Nured-din sent an army to protect Egypt from the Franks (Christians of the First Crusade), and Saladin served in it. In 1169 he was appointed as vizier of Egypt, acting as representative of Nured-din. When Nured-din died Saladin became sultan of Egypt.

Saladin was the finest Muslim warrior of his time. He extended his rule southwards by conquering Nubia (northern Sudan), Yemen and other parts of southern Arabia. After Nured-din's death he invaded Syria, took Damascus and in 1187 captured the Holy City of Jerusalem. The news of this aroused the religious feelings of the leaders of western Europe, who launched the Third Crusade to try to recapture the city. The Crusaders spent most of their energy and enthusiasm in besieging Acre, which resisted them for 2 years. Many of them returned home, and the rest, led by RICHARD I of England, could make no further headway against Saladin. In 1192 Saladin concluded a treaty with Richard which gave the Crusaders a coastal strip in Palestine, but kept Jerusalem in Muslim hands. A few months later Saladin died in Damascus.

SARGON II (died 705 BC), king of Assyria, raised his empire to its greatest period of power and wealth. He was the son of King Shalmaneser V, who died while besieging the Israelite city of Samaria in 722 BC. Sargon completed the siege and, as inscriptions found in the Assyrian city of Nineveh record, 'led away into captivity 27,290 people who lived there'. Sargon made Israel a province of Assyria, and colonised it with settlers from elsewhere in the empire. The colonists intermarried with Israelites from neighbouring territories, but developed their own form of the Jewish religion. This is how the Samaritans came to be regarded with dislike and suspicion by the Jews centuries later.

In 721 Sargon marched eastwards to fight against Babylon, which had just acquired a new king, Merodach-baladan. But he was defeated by the Babylonians' allies from neighbouring Elam, and had to retreat. Then came news that the people of Damascus, Gaza, and Hamath, backed by the Philistines, the remnants of the Israelites, and the Egyptians, had rebelled against Assyrian rule. At the battle of Raphia Sargon defeated a combined Egyptian and Philistine force under Pharaoh Osorkon. Sargon spent the next 10 years fighting attacks from the north of his huge empire. In 709 he again attacked Babylon, routed Merodach-baladan, and had peace on his eastern frontiers. He died a few years later, possibly fighting once more against the northern tribes; his son SENNACHERIB succeeded him.

Sargon, when he was not fighting, was a great builder of temples and palaces. His greatest work was the royal city of Dur-Sharrukin (Sargonsburg), a short distance north of Nineveh. It contained a palace standing on a 25 acre (10 hectare) brick platform.

SENNACHERIB (died 681 BC) succeeded his father, SARGON II, as king of Assyria in 705 BC. He did not have his father's political cunning, nor his military skill; he let his temper and enthusiasm run away with him. For the first 2 years of his reign he had peace; then Babylon and its neighbouring country Elam rebelled against him, and Sennacherib had to subdue them. He put a puppet king on the throne of Babylon, thus giving up his father's claim to the actual throne. The following year trouble broke out in the west, when the various kings of Phoenicia and Palestine all revolted against the rule of Assyria. Sennacherib rapidly subdued Phoenicia, the kings of Ammon, Moab and Edom all submitting before they were also attacked. Seeing a threat to Egypt, the Egyptians mustered a mixed force of Nubians, Ethiopians and Egyptians and moved forward to the attack. They were decisively routed.

The one remaining rebel was the king of Judah, Hezekiah, who was shut up inside the walls of Jerusalem where Sennacherib could not get at him. Finally Hezekiah agreed to terms, and the siege was raised on payment of tribute. An epidemic in the Assyrian camp seems to have helped Hezekiah to make peace.

While Sennacherib was busy in the west, Babylon rebelled again. Sennacherib pacified the region and put his own son on the throne in place of the puppet king. Six years later, Sennacherib launched a further expedition to stamp out the seeds of rebellion once and for all. A bloody battle in which both sides suffered heavy losses slowed Sennacherib down, but after a year's rest he again attacked Babylon. This time he razed the city to the ground, diverting the waters of a canal to flood the ruins. The king then returned in triumph to his own new capital, Nineveh, which he had rebuilt on a grandiose scale. The last years of Sennacherib are something of a mystery, but in 681 BC 2 of his sons murdered him while he was at worship. Another son, Esarhaddon, chased them out of Assyria and became king.

SHAH JAHAN (1592–1666) was the fifth Mughal emperor of India. The grandson of AKBAR THE GREAT, he succeeded his father, Jahangir, as emperor in 1628. At first he was a vigorous administrator, and during his reign the revenue doubled; but it appears that he over-taxed the peasants to pay for his splendid court, for many of them gave up farming because it did not pay.

Magnificence was Shah Jahan's ruling passion. He had 11 jewelled thrones, the most costly of which, the Peacock Throne, cost £1,000,000 at the value of sterling then. He encouraged the production of luxury goods such as carpets and shawls. He founded a new city, Shajahanabad, now part of Delhi, which was the centre both of his empire and of his opulence. The most famous of the buildings he had constructed is the Taj Mahal, the tomb at Agra of his beloved wife Mumtaz Mahal, who died in 1631.

Shah Jahan extended his empire southwards, and for a time made some conquests in the north-west. His reign was also noted for several severe famines, of which that of 1631 was much the worst, and for the extermination of a band of European desperadoes at the port of Hooghly. At the same time the English established a settlement at the little fishing port of Madras. Shah Jahan fell ill in 1656, whereupon his third son AURANGZEB, defeating his 3 brothers, made himself emperor. Shah Jahan ended his days a captive.

SOLOMON (*c.* 993 BC–933 BC) succeeded his father, DAVID, as king of Israel and Judah when he was not quite 20 years old. He was David's son by Bath-sheba, a woman whom David married after her husband was killed in battle. He was not the eldest of David's surviving sons, but his mother and Nathan, a prophet who acted as David's spiritual adviser, persuaded the dying king to name Solomon as his heir. Solomon's reign began with the repression of many discontented elements; thereafter his reign was peaceful. The only difficulties were caused largely by the king's extravagance.

Solomon was a statesman, where his father had been mainly a warrior. From this grew up the tradition that ascribes great wisdom to him. Solomon was careful to make advantageous treaties with neighbouring powers. An alliance with Egypt brought him a wife and the important trading city of Gaza. Alliances with the Phoenicians led to him receiving a percentage on their trading ventures: Phoenician merchants returning from India brought their goods up the Gulf of Aqaba to Elat, and then overland to the Mediterranean ports. From all this trading Solomon grew wealthy, but he spent as freely as he received. His court was a splendid one, its many courtiers being housed in a succession of magnificent palaces. Next to the palace in Jerusalem Solomon built a temple, inaugurated in about 953 BC. It made Jerusalem the spiritual centre of Israel as well as its temporal capital. Solomon, like his father, maintained a large harem, so large as to give rise to the legend that he had a thousand wives. They included, according to some traditions, Balkis, the queen of Sheba, though others say she returned to her own land (Yemen) astounded at Solomon's magnificence.

All this expenditure had to be paid for by heavy taxation. This led to considerable unrest, which after Solomon's death caused the break-up of his kingdom. Solomon's son Rehoboam succeeded him as king, but soon afterwards the northern tribes revolted under the leadership of Jeroboam, overseer of a forced-labour contingent. Thereafter the kingdom was split into Israel in the north and Judah in the south.

Many legends grew up about Solomon, who was supposed to possess magical powers and be able to talk to animals and birds. Several books are attributed to him, though he did not in fact write any of them. They include the Biblical books of *Proverbs*, *Ecclesiastes* and the *Song of Solomon*. The royal house of Ethiopia was said to be descended from Solomon and Balkis.

STEPHEN I (977–1038) founded the kingdom of Hungary. He was the son of Duke Geza, head of the Arpad family and leader of the Magyars, the leading Hungarian tribe. Geza became a Christian and had his son baptised at the same time as himself. At the age of 19 Stephen married a Bavarian princess, whose father later became the Holy Roman Emperor Henry II. A year later Geza died, and Stephen faced a rebellion by the eastern tribes of Hungary, who were still pagan.

For the next few years Stephen was busy suppressing the pagans, and converting them to Christianity. According to tradition, Pope Sylvester II sent him a crown, and in 1001 Stephen was crowned as Hungary's first king. He spent the rest of his life remodelling his kingdom on western, principally Germanic, lines, and in a fairly ruthless policy of conversion to Christianity. Such strong-arm methods, however, were typical of the age and place in which he lived. His last years were troubled about quarrels over the succession. In 1083 Stephen was canonised as a saint, and has been revered as his country's patron saint ever since.

SULEIMAN I, THE MAGNIFICENT (*c.* 1494–1566), was probably the greatest of the sultans of the Ottoman empire. He was the son of Sultan Selim I, whom he succeeded in 1520. To Turks, Suleiman is remembered as *Kanuni*, the 'lawgiver', because of the reforms both in the law and the administration of the empire which were carried out during his reign. In fact, Suleiman left much of the administration to his viziers, such as Ibrahim Pasha.

Suleiman was a proud and ambitious man, spending much of his energy in extending the frontiers of the empire in a series of brilliant campaigns. His first captures were Belgrade, in 1521, and the island of Rhodes, in 1522. Four years later, at the battle of Mohács, Suleiman crushed the Hungarians, whose king, Louis II, was killed while leading his disorderly army of peasants and nobility. Suleiman recognised John Zápolya of Transylvania, one of his subjects, as the new king. But Archduke Ferdinand of Austria also claimed the throne. Suleiman had to mount a new campaign to support Zápolya, during which he besieged Vienna. In 1533 he made peace with Ferdinand, who agreed to split Hungary with Zápolya and pay tribute to Suleiman.

The sultan formed an alliance with the French, enemies of the Austrian Habsburg rulers, and Turkish fleets ravaged the Mediterranean coast. But his main efforts were spent in major campaigns against Persia, from whom he conquered what is now the eastern part of Turkey and Syria.

Suleiman was completely under the influence of his concubine Roxelana, a beautiful slave from Russia. As a result, he had his legitimate sons Mustafa and Bayazid strangled with bowstrings so that Roxelana's son Selim could succeed him as sultan.

TAMERLANE (1336–1405), a Mongol conqueror, made himself master of an empire which stretched from India to Turkey. His name, *Timur i Leng*, means 'Timur the Lame'. He claimed to be a descendant of GENGHIS KHAN, and certainly had much of his dash and courage. Tamerlane was the son of a Tatar chief who lived near Samarkand, now in the Soviet Union. In 1361 he invaded the city, but failing to gain the promised support of other chiefs he took to the desert, where he had many adventures. By 1370 he had rallied massive support and was able to proclaim himself the ruler of Samarkand and an area of 250,000 square miles (400,000 sq km).

Such a kingdom was not enough for Tamerlane's ambition. Soon he began the first of 35 campaigns which were to bring him 27 crowns. By 1387 he had overrun Persia, Afghanistan, Azerbaijan, and Kurdistan, and turned his attention to Russia. He overthrew the Mongol kingdom known as the Golden Horde, which ran northwards from the shores of the Black and Caspian seas, and occupied Moscow. In 1398 the veteran ruler proposed to his chiefs an invasion of India. Sweeping aside their fears of the intervening rivers, mountains, and deserts, to say nothing of the fearsome elephants used by Indian armies, Tamerlane led a huge army, 92,000 strong, across the mountains of the Hindu Kush and the River Indus. Having routed the Indian forces, the Mongols proceeded to sack Delhi, and employed large numbers of the once-dreaded elephants to carry the booty back to Samarkand.

For his final campaign Tamerlane moved westwards and south against the Turks and the Egyptians, capturing Aleppo and Damascus. Still not satisfied, Tamerlane, now nearly 70, planned an invasion of China. He set out at the head of 200,000 veteran soldiers, but after marching for 300 miles (480km) he was taken ill from drinking too much iced water, and died.

Besides his martial qualities Tamerlane was a cultivated man, a keen student of science and history, fond of chess; but he was a despotic and ruthless ruler.

TIBERIUS (42 BC–AD 37), the second Roman emperor, came to the throne in AD 14 the most famous of Roman generals and died universally hated. He was the stepson of the emperor AUGUSTUS, whom his mother Livia Drusilla married in 38 BC, having been compelled to divorce her husband to do so. Under Augustus, Tiberius distinguished himself as a soldier, leading successful expeditions to the Euphrates and Germany, and conquering lands in central Europe. He got on well with his troops, but was not a ready talker in political and social circles. In 6 BC he defied Augustus and retired to live in Rhodes.

Eleven years later his life had changed dramatically. Augustus's heirs, his grandsons Lucius and Gaius, had died and the emperor adopted Tiberius as his son and heir. He was the only connection of Augustus with the experience and skill to take on the task of ruling the empire. By AD 13 Tiberius was virtually co-ruler, and when Augustus died the following year Tiberius was proclaimed emperor. He accepted his new honours with reluctance.

The reign of Tiberius began with the murder of Augustus's only surviving grandson, an uncouth young man named Agrippa Postumus who would have been a disaster had he become emperor. This cruel but necessary act, Tiberius maintained, had been ordered by Augustus on his deathbed. The new emperor carried out his duties with a grim conscientiousness, striving to follow the example of his predecessor and finding difficulty in formulating new ideas of his own when there were no precedents to follow. Under his rule the provinces in particular were well administered.

The blackest mark on Tiberius's reign was the series of treason trials which began in AD 16. The emperor seemed to see plots and plotters everywhere; if he was looking at the Senate he may well have been right. The Senate, incidentally, had to act as court for the trials. The first notable case was that of Gnaeus Piso, who was accused of poisoning Tiberius's nephew and heir, Germanicus. He was able to disprove this, but not another charge of inciting the troops against the emperor. Cornered, Piso committed suicide. Another senior statesman to face trial was Lucius Aelius Sejanus, suspected of conspiring to seize power. He was executed.

In 36 Tiberius retired to the island of Capri, never returning to Rome. His mental state was by now very disturbed and he obviously feared for his life, but he still retained his careful control of the administration. In 35 he named as his co-heirs his own grandson, Tiberius Gemellus, a boy of 16, and Germanicus's son, Gaius, nicknamed 'Caligula' (little boots) because of the military boots he wore as a small boy in an army camp. In 37 Tiberius died, and when the news reached Rome the crowds shouted 'Tiberium in Tiberim'—'throw his body in the Tiber'. Gaius succeeded him, and Gemellus was put to death.

Tiberius's full name was originally *Tiberius Claudius Nero*, but when Augustus adopted him he changed his name to *Tiberius Julius Caesar*. He was married first to Vipsania, but Augustus compelled him to divorce her and marry his own daughter, Julia, thus making Tiberius his son-in-law, if not son in fact.

TIGLATH-PILESER III (died 728 BC) was one of the greatest Assyrian conquerors. His name was originally *Pul*. He usurped the throne of Assyria in 745 BC, overthrowing the weak king, Assurnirari V. The new king's firm rule soon restored order in his country, sections of which were in revolt, and quelled its rebellious vassal states, particularly Babylon. He then set out to make the frontiers of Assyria safe, and to extend them. He began by driving back the Medes in the north-east, and then swept west-wards, subduing the whole of Syria in a 3-year campaign.

A few years afterwards there was a conspiracy of states in the Syria-Palestine region aimed at blocking further advances by

Tiglath-Pileser. It was led by Uzziah (Azariah), king of Judah. Tiglath-Pileser, recalled from a campaign in Armenia, swiftly broke up the conspiracy. In 734 the situation reversed. Uzziah's grandson, Ahaz, refused to join a new conspiracy against Assyria and was invaded by Israelite and Syrian armies. He appealed for help to Tiglath-Pileser, who seized the opportunity to capture Damascus, subdue other city-states, and occupy most of Israel. After this campaign Tiglath-Pileser returned to Babylon to settle a new rebellion, and annexed the land under his own rule.

TUTANKHAMUN (*c.* 1371 BC–1351 BC) was the son-in-law of the Egyptian pharaoh AKHENATEN, whose passion for religious reforms had led to a serious crisis in Egyptian political life. Tutankhamun became pharaoh at the age of 10. The real power lay in the hands of the priests of Amun and the army. Tutankhamun died at the age of 19 or 20, and it is possible that he was murdered.

His brief reign is comparatively unimportant, but what makes him famous is the discovery in 1922 of his tomb, intact with all its treasures in it. It is the only grave of a pharaoh to come down to us virtually unrobbed. Work on a pharaoh's tomb proceeded during his lifetime. The magnificence of Tutankhamun's tomb, accomplished in 10 years or less, shows what treasures there must have been in the tombs of pharaohs who lived longer. Most of the treasures are now in the Cairo Museum, but the boy-king's mummified body remains in its grave, in the Valley of the Kings at Thebes.

VESPASIAN (AD 9–79) was the ninth emperor of Rome. He was a well-educated man of a not very distinguished family; his father was a tax-collector, a member of the body known as *equites*, roughly equivalent to knights. He became a senator and a military leader of distinction, serving in Britain, Germany, Judaea and Thrace. He was a favourite of the emperor NERO until he made the mistake of leaving the room while Nero was singing, or—

possibly worse still—staying and falling asleep. Vespasian fled
from court for a while, but later regained favour sufficiently to be
appointed legate in Judaea. There he crushed the Jewish revolt
of 66–68.

In 68 Nero committed suicide and civil war broke out in Rome.
Successively Servius Sulpicius Galba, Aulus Vitellius and Marcus
Salvius Otho made themselves emperor. Otho had Galba murdered, but then committed suicide himself after being defeated
by Vitellius. Soon afterwards Vespasian was proclaimed emperor,
supported by most of the army. While Vespasian still held aloof,
staying in Italy, his supporters defeated and killed Vitellius in a
bloody battle in the streets of Rome.

The new emperor took up office in Rome in 70. At the age of
61 he still retained the rural shrewdness of his native central
Italian background. He was hard-working, lived a simple life and
always looked the countryman he was. A natural carefulness in
money matters earned him a largely undeserved reputation for
meanness.

He took over the imperial throne at a time when Rome's
finances were in a bad way, due to the extravagances of Nero and
the cost of the civil war. By dint of care in spending and heavy
taxation he managed to pull the imperial treasury out of debt, and
even accumulate a surplus, despite lavish spending on new building and the arts. He also tightened up discipline in the army,
which had become out of hand. When a young officer seeking
promotion came to him reeking of scent Vespasian refused him,
saying with an expression of disgust: 'I shouldn't have minded so
much if it had been garlic!'

His administration was formed partly of people with similar
backgrounds to his own: middle-class people, promoted into the
nobility. In this way he acquired assistants of real ability. His
rough humour did not appeal to some of his followers, but it
enabled him to turn into jokes many matters that might, taken
seriously, have led to tension and friction. Even on his death-bed
his wit did not leave him. 'Dear me,' he murmured, 'I must be

turning into a god!' When he had breathed his last his sorrowing subjects at once honoured him as such; he was only the third emperor to be deified.

Vespasian's full name was *Titus Flavius Vespasianus*. He married Flavia Domitilla, a lady of doubtful virtue, who bore him two sons Titus and Domitian. Both in turn became emperor after their father's death. Flavia died before Vespasian became emperor, and he spent the rest of his days with a former mistress of his youth, Caenis.

VICTOR EMMANUEL II (1820–1878), King of Sardinia, became the first king of a united Italy in 1861. He was the son of King Charles Albert of Sardinia, a kingdom that included not only the island of Sardinia but also the Piedmont area of north-western Italy. Victor Emmanuel was brought up strictly, and joined the Sardinian army.

In 1848, the 'Year of Revolutions' in Europe, the people of Milan, in Lombardy, rebelled against their Austrian rulers and sought aid from the liberal-minded Charles Albert. Piedmontese forces crossed the border into Lombardy, but in 1849 the Austrians decisively defeated them at the battle of Novara. Charles Albert abdicated, and his son became king. Victor Emmanuel made terms with the victorious Austrian commander, Josef Radetzky. These terms, which included the obligation to steam-roller them through the Sardinian parliament, have been much criticised; in the circumstances they were probably the best Victor Emmanuel could make.

In 1852, somewhat unwillingly, Victor Emmanuel appointed Count Camille Cavour, a Liberal dedicated to the unification of Italy, as his prime minister. Under Cavour's guidance Piedmont-Sardinia sent a contingent to fight in the Crimean War as allies of the Turks, French and British against the Russians; this gave Cavour a voice in the peace talks and a chance to raise Italian grievances. Later, Cavour made a secret deal with the emperor NAPOLEON III of France for a joint French-Piedmont war against

Austria. Part of the deal, which Cavour had to 'sell' to Victor Emmanuel afterwards, was that the king's 15-year-old daughter Clothilde should marry Napoleon's brother Jerome, a 37-year-old rake. War duly followed, but once Lombardy had been captured Napoleon made peace with Austria and persuaded Victor Emmanuel to agree. Cavour promptly resigned, but after a few months of less competent ministers, Victor Emmanuel appointed him premier again.

As payment to France for its support, Victor Emmanuel had to cede Nice and the duchy of Savoy to the French. However, soon after, with much negotiating from Cavour, the duchies of Parma, Modena and Tuscany in central Italy voted to become part of Piedmont-Sardinia. In 1860, encouraged by Victor Emmanuel, the Italian patriot Giuseppe Garibaldi led a force known as 'the Redshirts' which conquered the kingdom of the Two Sicilies—Sicily and the whole of southern Italy. At this moment, on the advice of Cavour, Victor Emmanuel led an army to annex most of the Papal States, which lay between southern Italy and the enlarged Piedmont. Most of Italy being now under one ruler, Victor Emmanuel was duly proclaimed King of Italy on 17 March 1861. Only 2 parts of Italy remained outside the new kingdom: Venezia in the north-east, still under Austrian rule, and Rome, ruled by the pope. In 1866 Italy made a secret treaty with Prussia; as allies they defeated Austria in a war lasting 7 weeks. Italy's prize was Venezia. However, Rome was protected by a garrison of French troops. In 1870 war between France and Prussia led to the withdrawal of the French forces and Victor Emmanuel marched into Rome and made it his capital. The pope, Pius IX, refused the terms offered by Victor Emmanuel, so both he and the popes who followed him remained 'prisoners of the Vatican' until 1929, when Pius XI finally agreed to much of the original settlement.

With the aid of a series of wise ministers, Victor Emmanuel spent the last 8 years of his life organising the new kingdom, which passed to the king's son, Umberto I, in a thriving state.

VICTORIA (1819–1901) had the longest reign of any British monarch. It was a reign which saw great changes in the British way of life, especially in technical and scientific progress, as well as the rapid expansion of the British empire. It was a period in which certain attitudes of mind developed that have given to the reign the name of the 'Victorian age'.

Victoria was the only child of George III's fourth son, Edward Duke of Kent. In 1817 the death of the king's only legitimate grandchild, Princess Charlotte, daughter of the Prince Regent (later George IV) left the country with no immediate heir to the throne. So three of George III's unmarried sons, the dukes of Clarence, Cambridge and Kent, all married in the hope of producing heirs. The Duke of Clarence succeeded to the throne in 1830 as William IV, when George IV died. His own children having died in infancy, Victoria was the heir to the throne. She learned how near to the succession she was at the age of 11, shortly before George IV died. Tearfully, she told her German governess, Baroness Louise Lehzen: 'I will be good.' By this precept she tried to live all her long life.

The Duke of Kent having died when Victoria was 8 months old, her mother, Mary Louise Victoria of Saxe-Coburg-Gotha, brought her up and hoped to become the power behind the throne. However, when the news of her accession was brought to the 18-year-old Victoria at 6am on 20 June 1837, she displayed a will of her own that put her ambitious mother firmly in her place.

During her first years Victoria leaned heavily on her first prime minister, Lord Melbourne. Although the young queen was trying to live up to her childhood ideal, she was at times thoughtless and, like all her family, was fond of pleasure. It became obvious that the sooner she married and secured further succession to the throne the better. The suggested candidate was her cousin, Prince Albert of Saxe-Coburg-Gotha, whom she had met when they were children. On 10 October 1839 Albert visited the English court. The queen loved him at once, and within 5 days she proposed to him. They were married in February 1840.

Albert was a handsome young man with strict notions of morality and duty. His influence over the young queen grew rapidly: he advised her on political matters and organised her life for her. He and Victoria had many relatives in the royal houses of Europe, so they were able to contribute their own unofficial diplomatic service to the country's government. Victoria, acting on her husband's advice, insisted on her right to be informed of current events by her ministers, and to give them her own views and advice.

The high standards of conduct both in private and in public life which Victoria and Albert set had 2 great effects. First, they re-established respect for royalty, which had declined sharply during the lifetime of George III's dissolute sons. Secondly, they influenced the behaviour and thinking of the British people, and though some of Victoria's subjects were hypocrites, who professed to be good while secretly being anything but so, the general standard of life rose. It is this moral attitude, more than anything else, that is the hallmark of the 'Victorian age'.

This happy period of Victoria's life came to a sudden end in December 1861, when Prince Albert died from typhoid fever. His last act of statehood was to redraft a government note to the United States over the kidnapping of 2 Confederate envoys from a British ship on the high seas. His action almost certainly prevented war between the two countries.

Albert's death left Victoria desolate. She suffered a nervous breakdown, and even after she recovered she spent much of her time in seclusion. Of the 2 parts of a British monarch's duties—the social and ceremonial on the one hand and the business and constitutional on the other—Victoria now carried out only the second. Her public appearances were reduced to the absolute minimum. In private she remained the autocrat she had become under Albert's tutelage. When her second son, Alfred, was offered the throne of Greece she not only forbade him to take it—her government fully concurring—but also acted to prevent Albert's brother Ernest, who had adopted Alfred as his heir, from taking the Greek throne himself. She was always disappointed in her eldest son, later Edward VII, a cheerful and pleasure-loving prince whom she kept firmly out of the political and constitutional limelight.

In 1876 Victoria was given the additional title of Empress of India. It was her own idea, prompted by the assumption by the King of Prussia, WILLIAM I, of the title of Kaiser (Emperor) of Germany. She grew more active at this time, a fact which may have been partly due to the influence of John Brown, a devoted Highland servant, who was about the only person who dared to speak his mind to the queen. After his death in 1883 she began to retreat into herself again. Even so, she never neglected her constitutional duties, reading masses of papers and discussing affairs with her ministers. With age, her personal popularity grew, and the celebrations of her golden jubilee in 1887 and diamond jubilee in 1897 were spontaneous and joyful. When she died, in the first few days of the twentieth century, her people felt that the world would never be the same again.

Victoria was not tall, but she had such a commanding presence that her family and ministers went in considerable awe of her. She had a beautiful speaking voice and on occasion a delightful smile.

WILLIAM I, THE CONQUEROR (*c.* 1027–1087), inherited the dukedom of Normandy from his father, and made himself King of England by force of arms. His actions changed the course of English history and played a major part in producing the England and its people of today.

William was born at Falaise in Normandy, the illegitimate son of Duke Robert I of Normandy and a girl named Herleve or Arlette, a tanner's daughter. Having no legitimate son, Robert named William as his heir, and William succeeded him as duke in 1035, while still a boy. The first years of his dukedom were a period of anarchy and murder, but the boy, already possessed of an iron will, survived, partly because there was in Normandy a strong tradition of ducal authority. The most serious rebellion against him came in 1047, but his overlord, the French king, Henry I, came to his rescue and helped him to win the battle of Val-ès-Dunes, which crushed the revolt. In 1051 William helped Henry to defeat Geoffrey Martel, Count of Anjou, who had taken the Norman city of Alençon. The people of Alençon greeted the besieging duke by beating hides and calling out 'Welcome to the tanner'. When he stormed Alençon William took his vengeance.

The growing power of William turned Henry of France against him. In 1054 Henry tried to invade Normandy but William defeated him most thoroughly at the battle of Mortemer. From then on, his power was undisputed. Before he was 27 years old he had achieved a reputation as one of the greatest generals of the day.

There were close ties between the court of Normandy and that of England: Robert's father had married the sister of Canute, the Danish king of England, while the current king of England, the Saxon Edward the Confessor, had spent 25 years in Normandy and was almost more Norman that English. Edward's mother, Emma, was a Norman princess, and through this link William had a claim, though a thin one, to the English crown. William's chief rival was Harold Godwinesson, Earl of Wessex and the most powerful man in England. In 1064 fate threw Harold into William's hands: he was shipwrecked on the French coast and held to ransom by the Count of Ponthieu. William asked for his release and entertained Harold royally. The 2 men, rivals for England, became personal friends. Under carefully concealed coercion, Harold was made to swear an oath to help William to the English crown.

Harold returned to England, where he ruled the country in the name of the dying Edward. When Edward finally died, the Witan, the English council, offered the throne to Harold in terms he could not refuse, oath or no. But that oath enabled William to mount an invasion of England under the guise almost of a holy war, with the blessing of the pope. Norman propaganda portrayed Harold as a perjured usurper. William appealed for help in this campaign, and mercenaries and adventurers flocked to his banner from all over France, Flanders, Italy and Spain. A fleet of ships was hurriedly built, and by the summer of 1066 all was ready for an attack across the English Channel.

William was greatly helped by a simultaneous attack by a rival claimant, King Harold Hardraada of Norway, supported by Harold of England's half-brother Tostig. The English demolished the Norwegian invasion, but then had to hurry to the south coast to meet William's attack. The Norman and Saxon armies, each of about 8,000 men, met on a ridge a few miles north of Hastings. At a general, Harold was William's peer. The fight lasted 8 hours, nearly 3 times as long as most battles of the time. At dusk Harold lay dead and William was master of the field.

The Saxons might have rallied, but they lacked a leader. On Christmas Day, 1066, William was crowned king in Westminster Abbey. Resistance continued in the north, but in 4 years William and his followers completed the Norman conquest of England, laying large parts of the north waste in the process. Over the next few years William confiscated most of the Saxon nobles' lands and gave them to his own followers, on strict terms of military service. Warned by experience in Normandy, he took care to split up each man's holdings, so that he would find it harder to organise his forces to rebel, and in any case each baron had to think nationally about his estates rather than regionally.

Having imposed a new Norman aristocracy on England, William kept as many of the old Saxon institutions and laws as he could. By this means he ensured continuity and also reduced the grievances of the conquered Saxons to the minimum. His government was firm and ruthless, but it brought peace to the land. As the anonymous compiler of the *Anglo-Saxon Chronicle* wrote: 'He was a very stern and violent man, so that no one dared to do anything contrary to his will . . . the good security he made in this country is not to be forgotten, so that any honest man could travel over his kingdom without injury with his bosom full of gold.' Though the Saxons groaned under William's taxes and mourned their thousands of dead, by 1075 it was they who supported the king against a rebellion of Norman knights.

William also encouraged the reform of the English Church, his homeland of Normandy being a stronghold of religion. On the material side, he ordered a survey of his new territories to find out exactly what he had conquered, and how much taxation he could levy on the land. The result, known ever since as the Domesday Book, was completed in 1086.

The Conqueror had 3 sons. The eldest, Robert, was heir to Normandy, later rebelling several times against his father. William was left the throne of England, and Henry, the youngest, a lump sum of money. William I died in 1087 from an internal injury sustained while riding on a campaign against the French. By 1106 William was dead, Robert a prisoner and HENRY I was ruler of both England and Normandy.

WILLIAM III (1650–1702) was stadtholder (ruler) of the Netherlands, and later King of England. He was the son of William II, Prince of Orange and stadtholder, and Mary Stuart, daughter of CHARLES I of England. Eight days before his birth his father died of smallpox, and the office of stadtholder, which was controlled by the Dutch parliament, the States-General, was suspended. This was possible because the provinces forming the Netherlands were nominally a federal republic. Although he was thus debarred from taking office, William was brought up with a view to becoming head of state at some future time.

His chance came when he was 21 when England and France mounted a joint attack on the Netherlands. In the face of this threat William was appointed captain-general, or commander-in-chief of the Dutch armed forces. A few weeks later he was proclaimed stadtholder as well. French armies quickly overran a great deal of the country, but William had the dykes breached to flood the land and halt the invaders. He held off the French while building up his military strength on land, and defeated the English navy at sea. By 1674 the English king, CHARLES II, was glad to make peace, and the French had withdrawn from most Dutch lands. Four years later the French too made peace.

In 1677 William strengthened the now friendly relationships with England by marrying Mary, daughter of Charles's brother James, heir to the English throne. James II became king on Charles's death in 1685, but soon fell out with his people because of his Roman Catholic faith. In 1688 a group of English statesmen sent a secret invitation to William to come to England and turn James out. When a son was born to James, interposing an heir between William's wife, Mary, and the English throne, a more urgent invitation was sent. On 15 November 1688, William landed in England with an army, and marched to London. James's troops refused to defend him, and rebellion flared all over the country. James fled the country with hardly a shot fired.

William, who still had no official status in England, summoned a Convention Parliament, which after much debate offered the crown jointly to William and Mary. Attempts to give the throne only to Mary met with a cold reception from William. William based his claim to the throne on the fact that he was the next heir after Mary's sister, Anne, who agreed to waive her claim. But from the English point of view the fact that William and Mary received the throne at the hands of a parliament established finally the supremacy of parliament over the crown.

The first years of the reign were spent subduing rebellions against the new rulers in Scotland and Ireland. James II landed in Ireland in 1689 with French troops, and was welcomed in Dublin with open arms. The following year William also landed in Ireland, and met James at the battle of the Boyne, in County Meath (now in the Republic of Ireland). William won a resounding victory and James fled to France. A hundred years later, Irish Protestants formed the Orange Society, named in honour of William, and they still hold annual parades on the anniversary of the battle. Scottish rebellion came to an end a year earlier, but some of the clan chiefs were very slow in taking the oath of allegiance. The chief of the Macdonalds of Glencoe delayed too long, and his clan enemies obtained an order from William for 'the extirpation of that den of thieves'. Members of the Campbell clan carried out the judicial murder by treachery. It is said that William signed the order without reading it, but he never punished the killers.

Between 1691 and 1697 William spent most of his time fighting on the Continent against the French, with whom Britain and the Netherlands had been at war since 1689. The Treaty of Ryswick in 1697 freed William to attend to home affairs in England—alone, for Mary II had died in 1694. But in the next few years it became apparent that the French king, LOUIS XIV, was still seeking to increase his power, hoping to take over Spain when the childless Charles II, its last Habsburg monarch died. William helped to form a Grand Alliance of England, the Netherlands, Austria, Prussia and other German states against France, but he died before the war came. The year before parliament had settled the succession to the throne, for William and Mary had no children. Mary's sister Anne was to inherit the crown, and after her the descendants of Sophia of Hanover, a daughter of JAMES I and VI.

As a boy, William was said to be lively and possessed great charm, but an unhappy upbringing made him cold and reserved; and he remained so all his life. His health was poor: he suffered from asthma and tuberculosis, which made him irritable. As a soldier he was brave and he looked after his men well. It is notable that despite his cold manner he kept the affections of his wife and of a small circle of close friends. His great skill lay in diplomacy, and an ability to feel his way in a difficulty to a successful result.

WILLIAM I (1797–1888), King of Prussia, became the first kaiser (emperor) of a united Germany. As a child he saw his country humiliated at the hands of NAPOLEON I, and before the end of Napoleon's career he was fighting in the Prussian army against him. An army career, coupled with a natural hard-headedness, made him conservative and resistant to all the winds of change that blew across Europe in the 'Year of Revolutions', 1848. He had to go into exile for a while.

William's father, Frederick William III, died in 1840, leaving the throne to William's elder brother, Frederick William IV, an incurable romantic. In 1857 a stroke deprived the king of his reason, and William, who had returned to Prussia, ruled as regent from 1858 until the king died in 1861.

A serving soldier all his life, William was a supporter of and supported by the *Junkers*, the class of rich landowners from which the Prussian army drew most of its officers. He tried, and failed, to secure an increase in the size of the army, and in 1862 faced abdication. At that moment he found the man to serve his purpose: Otto von Bismarck, a Junker diplomat. Bismarck became prime minister, soon finding ways and means of circumventing the Prussian parliament and securing the military forces William desired. Bismarck set out to make Prussia powerful. He began by wresting the duchies of Schleswig and Holstein from Danish rule in 1864, helped by Prussia's chief rival, Austria. He then engineered a quarrel with Austria over the future ownership of the 2 duchies. In the Seven Weeks' War of 1866 William commanded the Prussian armies which defeated the Austrians at the battle of Sadowa. He allowed himself to be used by Bismarck in the manoeuvrings which led to the Franco-Prussian War of 1870–71. In this he again led his armies, and saw France crushed in 4 swift battles. Prussia gained the French provinces of Alsace and Lorraine, but more important it also gained the allegiance of all the other German states, except Austria. More manoeuvrings by Bismarck resulted in William being proclaimed German emperor in the Hall of Mirrors at Versailles in January 1871.

The remainder of William's reign was master-minded by Bismarck. The new emperor supported his minister, now chancellor, faithfully in all his policies. In 1888 he died, leaving the throne to his elder son, Frederick III, who, unfortunately, survived him by only a few months, the throne then passing to

WILLIAM II, son of Frederick and his wife Victoria, daughter of Britain's queen VICTORIA.

WILLIAM II (1859–1941) was the third and last Emperor (Kaiser) of Germany. His father was Prince Frederick, son of William I, and for a few months in 1888 himself emperor. His mother was Victoria, eldest daughter of England's queen VICTORIA. Dislocation of his arm at birth left it permanently withered. Not so his pride, which was always considerable: Queen Victoria commented on it when he was only 5 years old. He became an army officer in 1879, which did nothing to lessen his arrogance. By the time he came to the throne in 1888 he was convinced of his own divine right to rule, which when combined with a restless energy made him a dangerous person to lead a country like Germany.

The new emperor did not get on at all well with his uncle, the future Edward VII of Britain, but like most of his family he was in awe of his grandmother. She, however, was not at all impressed by his arrogant ways, and wrote to her prime minister, Lord Salisbury: 'We have always been very intimate with our grandson and nephew and to pretend that he is to be treated *in private* as well as in public as "his Imperial Majesty" is *perfect madness!*'

William began his reign by quarrelling with Otto von Bismarck, the chancellor who had helped to create the German empire, and dismissed him in 1890. The chancellors who succeeded Bismarck had neither the strength nor the skill of the 'Iron Chancellor', and much of the policy of Germany was dictated by its hot-headed young emperor. Half-hearted attempts to increase democratic government in Germany came to nothing. Owing to the system of government then in force, the strongest political party, the Social Democrats, was underrepresented in the Reichstag (parliament); the Reichstag had no way of controlling the ministers; the ministers could not control the emperor; and nobody had any control over the army. Meanwhile German industrial growth had led to an over-production of steel, so the steel industry was subsidised by building a large number of warships. The size of the new German navy, for which there was no real need for defence purposes, was regarded by Britain as a direct threat.

William's many interventions in foreign affairs were often tactless in the extreme. In 1896 he sent a telegram of congratulations to President Kruger of the Transvaal after the failure of an unauthorised British raid on his territory, an act which antagonised the British. In 1908 he gave an interview to the correspondent of the British newspaper *The Daily Telegraph* in which he set out his views on Anglo-German relations in hot-headed terms. His intention was to improve Anglo-German relations, but the only result was that his ministers, headed by Prince Bernhard von Bülow, compelled him to announce that he would 'respect his constitutional obligations'—a humiliation which led to William dismissing von Bülow 3 years later.

The Germans engineered 2 'confrontations' with France over Morocco, in 1905 and 1911, in which they claimed rights in North Africa. Each time they had to back down, and William regarded these 2 diplomatic defeats as personal humiliations. By this time the real rulers in Germany were the army. In 1914 the quarrel between Austria and Serbia over the assassination of the Austrian Archduke Francis Ferdinand brought a pledge of support for Austria from William, and led automatically to war between Germany and Serbia's allies, Russia and France.

Although he was technically supreme commander of the German armies, William had to leave the running of the war to his generals. He spent most of his time at army headquarters or moving from one part of the battle front to another. Gradually he lost all support and power, so much so that it became obvious in October 1918 that Germany would have to ask for peace terms, and William would have to abdicate. He did so with reluctance, and slipped away secretly over the border into the neutral territory of the Netherlands. He was given political asylum and an estate at Doorn, in Utrecht, and there he stayed, in seclusion, until his death in 1941.

BRIEF BIOGRAPHIES
Theodore Rowland-Entwistle and Jean Cooke

FAMOUS COMPOSERS

The composers important in the history of western music from the thirteenth century to the present day—the obvious great names, such as Bach, Beethoven, Handel, Mozart, Haydn and Brahms, as well as less well known composers whose music is frequently played: those who are important in the musical development of their own country, such as Victoria, Villa-Lobos and Nielson; and leading modern musicians including Berio, Britten, Ives, Boulez and Musgrave.

FAMOUS EXPLORERS

Brief accounts of the lives of those explorers whose journeys have contributed to our knowledge of the world in which we live. The entries range from the sophisticated modern explorations of such men as Richard Byrd, Vivian Fuchs, and Wally Herbert, to the romance of such figures as Richard Burton who wandered, disguised and at the risk of his life, through the streets of Mecca; from Francis Drake and Theodore Roosevelt for whom exploration was only a part of their lives, to Robert Scott, Robert Burke and William Wills who died attempting to conquer the unknown.

*   *   *

THE QUEENS OF ENGLAND
Barbara Softly

England's history has been as much influenced by her Queens as by her Kings. But we know far less about most of them.

This handy reference book provides the basic facts and dates for each First Lady—from Matilda, wife of William the Conqueror, right through to Elizabeth II.